# KOBE BRYANT
## THE GAME OF HIS LIFE

D0047889

JEFFREY SCOTT SHAPIRO
&
JENNIFER STEVENS

REVOLUTION PUBLISHING™

Published by Revolution Publishing, New York, New York.

Cover Photograph © Reuters New Media Inc / CORBIS
Designed and Typeset by Pierre Blondin

ISBN: 0-9748684-1-8

Printed in the United States of America.

February 2004

10 9 8 7 6 5 4 3 2 1

# CONTENTS

# Authors' Note

The information contained in Chapters 1 & 10 is a recreation of events reported by the alleged victim to police investigators, prosecutors and close friends when she encountered Kobe Bean Bryant on the night of June 30, 2003. Multiple sources have confirmed that Bryant's version of events are virtually no different from the alleged victim's, with the exception of the issue of consent and force. In Bryant's version to police investigators, the alleged victim did not tell him, "no," at any time during their sexual encounter.

One source close to the investigation described the case as being "about two words—yes and no." Otherwise, the source said, there was virtually no difference in the versions as relayed by the alleged victim and Bryant.

The alleged victim's name has been changed to Lilly Fuller to honor the journalistic covenant to shield the identities of alleged victims of sexual assault. In Chapter 16, the name Kristina Kelley has been used to protect the woman's true identity at her request. These names are fictitious and in no way are meant to represent any person, living or dead.

The remainder of the information contained in this book is the result of six months of extensive investigation and research by a small cadre of journalists from different locations across the United States, all of which has been carefully documented. The name "Jennifer Stevens" is a pen-name used at the request of those reporters other than the primary author. The authors' investigation encompassed journalistic research and interviews that were conducted in multiple locations in California, Colorado, Florida, Massachusetts, New York and Oregon.

Multiple attempts were made to interview Kobe Bryant including a formal request submitted to his attorneys in Denver, Colorado. Other attempts were made to contact Bryant personally at Staples Center in Los Angeles, at his training center in El Segundo, CA and at the Los Angeles Lakers private jet at LAX Airport during times when he was present at those locations. None were successful.

None of the sources who were interviewed for this book on the record, off the record or on background have been paid or compensated at any time, nor will they be paid or compensated at any time in the future.

As of this writing, it is important to note that Kobe Bryant has not been convicted of any crime and no sexual assault has been proved to have occurred.

# 1

## ROOM 35

Lilly Fuller crossed the threshold of Room 35 onto the hallway's plush maroon carpet. From there, she quickly made her way to the elevator, stepped in, and punched the button that would send her back on her way to the lobby of the exclusive Cordillera Lodge and Spa. As the elevator shuddered, she reflected on what had happened.

He had come into the hotel and greeted everyone as if he had done it a thousand times before. He was staying under the name Javier Rodriguez, which sounded foreign to her, and yet wasn't as strange as his real name. Lilly didn't know much about basketball and didn't care much for sports; the name "Kobe Bryant" had never passed her lips.

Celebrities were common at the Cordillera and when they first arrived, they were often shown to their rooms without a formal check-in. The staff had been trained to respect the privacy of the well-heeled. Lilly had been asked to escort him to Room 35, an isolated part of the hotel detached from the lobby, and, like an attentive concierge, she did what she was asked. She also had an envelope from the Property Division for him; it wasn't uncommon for management to advertise their luxury vacation homes to some of the wealthier guests. On the envelope was a label that read, "Mr. & Mrs. Bryant."

On the way to the room, Bryant seemed to take an interest in her. "That's a nice tattoo," he said, pointing to the small flower on her left ankle. Lilly and some of her friends had all agreed to get the tattoo as a way of honoring a friend who'd died earlier that year.

As they walked, Bryant's bodyguards began chatting with her as well and she thought the whole situation a little odd. Once they reached Room 35, Bryant's bodyguards began setting up their gear. While they were busy, Bryant took her aside. Touching her forearm, he whispered, "Listen, do you think you can show me around a little later? Can you come back, if you don't mind?" Lilly wasn't that surprised by the request. Many of the Cordillera guests asked for tours of the resort and it was a courtesy the hotel extended to everyone, celebrities and non-celebrities alike. She smiled and nodded.

Once she had escorted him and his companions to their rooms, she immediately returned to the lobby where she took her post next to the front doors. Just outside, in a small corridor that housed the hotel's entrance was her friend, Bobby Pietrack, the 19-year-old bellman with whom she'd attended Eagle Valley High School. Pietrack sat alone at a small podium with stacks of brochures advertising local attractions. It was already 10:15 p.m. and Lilly had just 45 minutes left on her shift. She had wanted to go home and get some sleep. But when someone asked for a tour, that was her job, and she really didn't mind. Anyway, it was a way to get out of the monotonous lobby and to interact with someone new.

She'd always been outgoing and loved to learn about new people. In this case, though, she didn't know much about Kobe Bryant. She did know, however, that he was someone her friends looked up to, so it would be fun to tell them she'd met him.

She happily returned to his room and knocked on the door.

Minutes later, as they walked through the hotel, Bryant seemed calm and self-possessed. He smiled at her as she described the hotel's features, and although he appeared to be listening, he was clearly distracted and thinking of something else. Even though his eyes were on her, she found herself wondering if he heard a single word. She showed him the downstairs area by the massage room and salon, and then took him outside to the pool, where he noticed that the Jacuzzi had been closed for the evening.

The two walked back toward the lobby, Lilly thinking her job was done and that she could finally go home for the evening.

When the two arrived back at the lobby, Bobby Pietrack wandered outside to the veranda where the NBA star and his escort were chatting. As a college basketball player, Pietrack found a conversation with Bryant tremendously exciting. After a few minutes Pietrack left the veranda to help another guest and Bryant turned to Lilly and asked if she could help him get back to his room.

She looked at him askance. Was he being serious? There was nothing to it, she thought. She thought about the fact that Bryant must spend his whole life in hotels and they must all blend together, so she looked at the clock and nodded. As they started back to his room, he asked her a question.

"So, do you have a boyfriend?"

The question caught Lilly off guard; she didn't know what to say. Her last boyfriend, Johnray Strickland, had attended the University of Northern Colorado, where she went to school. They'd only dated a month or so. He was a nice guy, but once the summer started he didn't keep up with her phone calls and eventually the two just drifted apart. She wondered if she would see him when she returned.

Before Johnray, she'd dated Matthew Herr, a local boy she'd gone to high school with in Gypsum. The two dated for nearly three years and she had expected that they would get married after graduation. Instead, the relationship ended, and Lilly found herself confused and abandoned. She had cared about Matt, and she was hurt. She avoided her feelings by trying to live her life like every other college student, making friends, going to parties and immersing herself in her studies. And now, suddenly, she had somehow earned the interest of a famous sports celebrity. She was mystified.

Lilly considered herself an intelligent young woman and her friends had often told her that she was going to amount to something. Deep down inside, she wasn't sure that was true, but she had hoped she could do something of substance with her life. The previous fall, she had traveled to Texas with her friend, Lindsey McKinney, to try out for television's on-air competition, *American Idol*. Lilly had a good voice, and many who knew her said she sounded as beautiful as she looked. Of the 3,000 who showed up for the try-outs, however, Lilly wasn't chosen a finalist.

Standing tall at 5-feet-9 inches, the college freshman had porcelain white skin and an athletic build. She wore her long blonde hair parted in the middle, and it cascaded down across her shoulders. Her blue eyes were piercing, and yet her smile conveyed a sense of naiveté, innocence and trust.

Interestingly, Bryant wasn't too far removed from that same naiveté and innocence himself. As a youngster, he had spent his formative years in Italy while his father, Joe Bryant, was wrapping up his professional basketball career. Kobe (named after the local steak house in King of Prussia, PA) was the gangly, black American kid who was treated as an outsider—if not for his painful shyness then for his almost otherworldly basketball skills. Bryant viewed his association with others through the multifaceted prism of basketball. Dates with girls consisted not of fooling around in the back row of the local movie theater, but of sitting in the living room with his parents and his date watching videotapes of his own games.

In his fitful, early NBA seasons, a teen on his own in the company of world-weary veterans, Bryant still didn't have much of a social life. When anyone inquired about the dating game, his response was brief and to the point: "Basketball is my girlfriend."

And once again, when he did date, the young lady would likely find herself in front of a television watching tapes with Kobe's parents, Joe and Pam Bryant, sitting a few feet away. It was an episode of *Ozzie and Harriet* in Pacific Palisades, with Kobe cast as Ricky, the precocious, abundantly gifted son, and basketball the main storyline. What it was not was a prescription for a well-rounded youngster.

Lilly was still trying to figure out how to answer Bryant's question when his smooth, cool voice interrupted her musings.

"You know, a beautiful girl like you should really have a boyfriend," he said with a smile. Lilly laughed nervously. She was confused. Was he just flirting or was he really hitting on her?

Bryant continued. He mentioned how toned her body was. He said she looked nice. Lilly looked down at herself. She had been wearing a simple black dress and a professional black blazer. She wondered what he wanted. She'd never thought of herself as particularly attractive.

"You're a nice height and a nice shape," he added.

Lilly thanked him for the compliment.

"Did you ever play any sports?" he asked.

Lilly told him that she'd played a little basketball when she was younger and Bryant began telling her about his recent knee injury. Although she had played the sport in her childhood, she wasn't impressed by athletes of any kind. She wanted to be a singer, and if there was a God, she would surely land the lead in her favorite Broadway musical, "Les Miserables."

Finally, they reached Bryant's room. It was getting late and her shift was almost over. To her surprise, Bryant opened the door and pointed inside. "Would you like to come in for a minute?"

Lilly paused. Normally, she wouldn't have entertained such an idea. Then she remembered the envelope she'd been asked to deliver. It was addressed to "Mr. & Mrs. Bryant." He was married. There was no way he was coming on to her. It was all in her head. If anything, he was probably trying to give her ego a boost. After all, just because she didn't really know who Mr. and Mrs. Bryant were didn't mean that *he* knew that. He probably figured that his comments would make her feel good about herself. Maybe he missed his wife and was just lonely. Maybe he just wanted to talk. Whatever the reason, Lilly knew that her friends would be excited to hear that she had hung out with a famous basketball player. She smiled.

"Okay," she said.

Bryant followed her inside. She looked around at a room she'd seen dozens of times. Suddenly the door shut behind her. For some reason, at that moment, Lilly remembered there was no one else on the entire floor.

\* \* \*

Lilly snapped out of her flashback as the elevator doors opened. It had happened. It had happened and now she would have to live with it. It was over. She could go home. She could go home and pretend like none of this ever happened. She walked out into the lobby where she saw a familiar face.

Bobby Pietrack was sitting on the couch chatting with a couple of Cordillera regulars. She motioned to him that something was wrong. Her eyes were watery and there was a look of shock on her face. On top of that, her dress was slightly askew and her blazer was wrinkled and out of place. Pietrack asked her what was wrong. She tried to speak but couldn't.

Finally, once the two were out in the parking lot, she grabbed his arm and began to tell him what had happened. Pietrack's eyes widened. He couldn't believe it.

Pietrack didn't know it at the time, but his willingness to listen to Lilly's account of what happened would position him as the prosecution's "outcry witness," a term commonly used to describe the first person to come into contact with an alleged victim after they've been attacked. In the coming months, the young man's credibility, which was considered untouchable in the Eagle community, would prove critical to the prosecution's case against Bryant.

It was already 11:15 p.m. and time to clock out. Despite all that had happened, Lilly didn't want a ride. She just wanted to go home in her own car. Pietrack vowed to follow her home to make sure she arrived safely in Eagle, about 15 miles up the road. As Lilly slouched to her car, she felt stunned. The turbulence of what she had just experienced contrasted sharply with the serenity of an otherwise peaceful evening.

The drive to the base of the hill seemed to take an eternity. Lilly gripped the steering wheel. As she drove, she tried hard to concentrate on the road ahead. It was windy and she could easily make a mistake and drive off the hill. Finally, she reached the gatehouse and turned onto Squaw Creek Road. In her rearview mirror, she could see Pietrack's headlights.

It was hard for her to come to terms with what had happened. An hour ago, she was simple Lilly, a 19-year old college freshman with her whole life ahead of her.

Before long, she would be accused of systematically trying to destroy the career of one of sports' greatest and most legendary players. Despite the accusations made against her, the fact of the matter was that before that night, Lilly Fuller hardly even knew who Kobe Bryant was.

He had hugged her first and then kissed her. She had tried to leave, but he blocked the door. Standing directly in her path with his arms extended, Bryant looked hurt.

He acted as if it was an honor. An honor? Is that what it was supposed to have been? She tried to hold back her tears. His arrogance was almost too much to believe. She had just wanted to tell her friends how much fun it had been to meet someone she knew they admired. If only she hadn't been working that night. If only she hadn't taken him on the tour. If only . . . .

Finally, she reached the base of the road. Pietrack continued to follow her. On her left she could see the stream that ran between Edwards and Eagle where she lived. She had grown up in that small town that housed a tiny population of 3,000. Lilly wasn't the kind of girl who knew a whole lot about city life, professional athletes or the American justice system. In time however, she would learn.

As she drove she quickly tapped the buttons to her cell phone. Her former boyfriend, Matthew Herr, was confused and stunned as he listened to her story. It had been a while since he and Lilly had dated, but he was horrified about what he was hearing. With her voice trembling, Lilly told him, step by step, everything that had happened.

She soon arrived at the Eagle town limits, where she reached the turnabout that led to the tiny downtown area. As usual, as it was every Monday night, the streets were silent and deserted. The town's main street, Broadway, hosted a restaurant, a bar, a coffee shop, one bank and the town hall. Upstairs in the town hall was a small police department with a dozen officers. Finally, Lilly reached home. Pietrack said goodnight to her and she went upstairs.

When Pietrack arrived back home, he immediately tried waking his father.

"Dad," Pietrack whispered, as he lightly shook his father. "Dad, you have to wake up."

"What?" Pietrack's father said quietly, not quite sure if he was awake or dreaming.

"Lilly was raped tonight at the hotel."

Pietrack's father said nothing.

"She was raped by Kobe Bryant—you've got to wake up."

Pietrack's father, sure he was dreaming, simply told his son, "I know this isn't happening so I'll see you in the morning."

Bobby was unsure of what to do and went back to his bedroom. Two minutes later Mr. Pietrack walked into Bobby's room.

"Did that just really happen?" he asked. "Did you just come in and tell me that Lilly was raped?"

Bobby, who was relieved that his father had finally come around, relayed Lilly's story to him. The older Pietrack was now deeply concerned and told his son to get Lilly on the phone immediately.

After listening to her, the elder Pietrack ordered Lilly not to take a shower and suggested she tell her story to the police. They would know how to handle it. Lilly did as she was told and didn't take a shower or wash up. Instead she went to sleep and waited until morning.

While she slept through the early morning hours, Kobe Bryant was waiting in the Cordillera lobby until 6:30 a.m. Lilly had misled him into thinking that her shift lasted from 7 a.m. to 3 p.m. that day, and Bryant was sitting in the lobby by himself.

When Lilly had bolted from Bryant's room, she had convinced him that she would be coming back, that she simply left to clock out. As she was scurrying down the hallway, Bryant went back into his room and called his wife, Vanessa. After 20 minutes, when Lilly hadn't returned, Bryant went to the lobby to look for her.

When he was told she had left for the evening, he nodded and looked out into the black Colorado night. He paced the lobby for several minutes and then accepted an offer from a Cordillera staffer to teach him how to play chess. Eventually, he went back up to his room and ordered a pay-per-view movie.

When the early-shift bellman came to work the next morning at 6:30, he noticed Bryant sitting alone in the empty lobby looking fidgety. He was still wearing the blue track pants and white T-shirt he'd been wearing the night before.

* * *

When Lilly woke, it was already late in the morning. She picked up her cell phone and called work. She was scheduled to be there from 11 a.m. to 7 p.m.—not 7 a.m. to 3 p.m., as she told Bryant. When her manager, Gabe Ericson received the news that she couldn't come in because she was "sick," he became angry and she was forced to hang up on her unsupportive employer. She didn't need a conflict now; she just wanted to talk to her mother.

She knew her mom was meeting a friend for lunch, so her cell phone would likely be on. When her mother answered, Lilly apologized for not having called earlier and told her that something bad had happened. When asked what it was, Lilly hesitated. Then she asked her mother to come home right away because there was something important she had to talk to her about. When her mother arrived home, the two sat down on Lilly's bed. Lilly turned to her and simply said, "I was raped." Then, carefully, after taking a deep breath, she went on, "I was raped—I was raped by Kobe Bryant."

Her mother was silent for a moment and then began screaming, "Oh, my God. Oh, my God, *oh, my God!*"

Still frantic, Lilly's mother called 911. Before long two investigators, Detective Doug Winters and Deputy Marcia Rich from the Eagle County Sheriff's Department, arrived at the Fuller home.

"Do you understand how serious this is—the allegations you're making?" Winters asked Lilly.

She nodded. After talking a while at her house, Winters and Rich collected the clothes Lilly had worn the night before from her bedroom floor. They demanded that she immediately accompany them into town.

As they stepped outside her two-story wood-frame home, Lilly looked up at the clear blue sky. It was a warm July 1, and she would spend most of the day answering questions about the worst experience of her life.

After an hour-long, taped interview at the Eagle County Sheriff's Office, the two investigators drove Lilly to the Glenwood Springs Hospital. There, she would endure an uncomfortable four-hour rape-kit process—something that she would prefer to forget when it was over.

"They did everything you wouldn't want someone to do," she later told her close friend, Starlene Bray.

When she arrived home, she crawled into bed and tried not to think about what had happened. It wouldn't be until the next day that her father would point out an abrasion on her neck where Bryant had grabbed her. She hadn't noticed it until then, but the contusion reminded her of his grip; he was strong, and it had been impossible to pry his hand away. She shuddered at the thought of it. Somehow, she would have to put it out of her mind.

The next couple of weeks were a blur. Her family had already scheduled a vacation to the Pacific Northwest and she was able to escape the all-too-familiar surroundings of Eagle County. While staying at her relative's, she spent her days in a fog. Everything seemed surreal. Nothing seemed vivid or lifelike enough to wake her from her stupor. And then one night, as she was watching the TV news, she was jolted awake.

Lilly Fuller knew that when the world learned Kobe Bryant was being charged with rape, the story would make the news. What she hadn't anticipated was that it would become a story that would haunt her for months to come. As she watched the TV now, the news crawl at the bottom of the screen announced Bryant's arrest. Lilly had expected it. Only a few hours before, Eagle County District Attorney Mark Hurlbert had called to let her know it was coming.

A week later, when she returned home to Eagle, she found more than a dozen reporters holding vigil at her front door. While her parents politely asked them to leave, Lilly hid in her bedroom upstairs. She wanted nothing to do with the media. She didn't want the attention. Just like Bryant, she just wanted her life back.

# 2

## UNDER SUSPICION

Thirty-six minutes past midnight on July 1, Kobe Bryant ordered a pay-per-view movie in what was about to become the most famous hotel room in America, a luxury suite in a remote corner of the exclusive Lodge and Spa at Cordillera.

Nothing on Bryant's movie menu card could have been as gripping, unpredictable and melodramatic as what had happened in that well-appointed hotel room, and what was about to unfold in the days, weeks and months to come.

Sometime after the movie had run its course, Bryant wrestled with sleep. He was due to undergo surgery on his right knee later that morning at the Steadman Hawkins Clinic in nearby Vail. During the Los Angeles Lakers' unsuccessful drive toward what would have been a fourth straight NBA title, their all purpose, all-universe guard had played valiantly, despite a painful, damaged knee and an injured right shoulder that would also require surgery. Even though eventual champion San Antonio foiled his team in the Western

Conference semifinals, Bryant's reputation continued to soar. He was widely hailed as the sport's most spectacular performer.

The Steadman Hawkins Clinic was a popular destination for big-name athletes like John Elway, Dan Marino, Monica Seles, and other notables in need of repair and specialized treatment. Bryant wasn't the only celebrity in surgery at the clinic that day. Hunter S. Thompson, who brought "gonzo" and other new and colorful terms to journalism with his eclectic rantings, was having back surgery, unaware of the arrival of an even bigger name from Los Angeles. In yet another bizarre coincidence, Phil Jackson, Bryant's celebrated coach with the Lakers, was encamped a few miles away during a stopover on a motorcycle excursion.

It would have ruined Jackson's trip had he known of Bryant's presence at the clinic. The two had butted heads many times before over the player's headstrong ways, mainly about his refusal to commit himself to the community-of-team that Jackson preached so fervently. Kobe, it would be revealed later, had not communicated his decision to team management to have the surgeries.

Understandably, the Lakers' front office executives, who were still accepting plaudits for their twin free-agency signings of superstars Karl Malone and Gary Payton, were beside themselves when they learned of Bryant's knee surgery. In L.A., Bryant performed in the company of several of the most respected surgeons and physicians in professional sports—notably Dr. Steve Lombardo, the team orthopedist. Yet Bryant, ever the rebel, had trekked to Colorado to have his knee cleaned out.

Returning to his hotel room in mid-afternoon, following the surgery, Bryant was noticeably limping. He spent the evening in his room, twice ordering room service.

At 11:30 p.m., he heard a knock on the door. When Bryant opened it, he found himself looking into the eyes of a pair of Eagle County Sheriff's investigators who said they needed to ask him a few questions. Bryant, whose body-guards, Michael Ortiz and Troy Laster, were usually in the vicinity, were also being interrogated by officers in the parking lot.

Meanwhile, in Room 35, the two detectives pulled out an audio recorder and began asking Bryant a list of questions. One was whether he had sex the prior evening with a woman who worked at the hotel. Bryant, who took a deep breath, told them that he had not. One of the investigators, treading lightly, told Bryant that he was sensitive to the precarious position of the married athlete. However, DNA tests would eventually confirm whether he'd had sexual relations with Lilly Fuller or not. Nodding silently, Bryant told the detectives what had happened. As he explained his story, he was breathing hard and wishing he'd never come to Colorado for knee surgery, or any other reason. Bryant's story mirrored most of what Lilly had told investigators. When one of the detectives asked him whether or not Lilly had ever said, "no," Bryant hesitated and said nothing. The detectives in the room sat motionless.

"You're not answering the question," one of them said.

"I'm thinking," Bryant said, slightly annoyed.

Exhaling a deep breath and looking down at his sneak-ers, Bryant made a variety of frustrated facial expressions and then, after 30 seconds of pondering the question, he responded.

"It was consensual," he said.

"What's that mean?" one of the detectives asked, getting frustrated.

Bryant said nothing, looking at the two men before him.

The detective firmly reiterated the question. "Did she ever say 'no'?"

Bryant paused. "No," he said quietly.

A dead silence fell over the room and the investigators looked at one another. To them, Bryant's evasiveness was deeply troubling. Two or three seconds of silence was perhaps normal, but 30 seconds of silence was deafening under the circumstances. For Bryant to have waited that long and then still not flatly denied the allegation, instead saying, "it was consensual," told investigators that Lilly had likely said, "no," but that in Bryant's mind, "no" could have meant "yes."

Later, when the prosecution listened to the tape-recorded interview, they would repeatedly time the gap between the detective's question and Bryant's response. Hurlbert was convinced that Bryant's silence spoke volumes about what had really happened and he was optimistic that a jury would feel the same way.

The two investigators asked Bryant not to leave the hotel. When they returned two hours later, they were armed with a warrant to collect evidence from his room.

At 2:30 a.m. on the morning of July 2, the superstar was taken to Valley View Hospital in Glenwood Springs, a trip of 52 miles. Shortly after 3 a.m. Bryant provided DNA samples at the hospital. Another facility, The Vail Valley Medical Center, had been closer to the Lodge and Spa at Cordillera by about 30 minutes, but an effort was being made to protect Bryant's privacy by taking him the distance to Glenwood Springs.

While Bryant was being transported to Glenwood, other investigators remained behind at Cordillera, collecting printouts of Bryant's room charges and phone records. One investigator noticed that at 11:13 p.m., almost immediately after Lilly Fuller said she'd left his room, Bryant had called his wife in Newport Beach. Hotel employees were urged not to speak publicly about the incident and management quickly established a policy in which those who did talk to the press were summarily fired.

At 3:30 a.m., Bryant's three bodyguards loaded into a taxi van at the Lodge and Spa at Cordillera. They were described by the driver as "nervous and anxious." One of the men told the driver, Terry O'Brien of Vail, that they were off to pick up "a friend having the worst day of his life." It would be only the beginning.

Picking up Bryant at the hospital, the three men had their driver take them to the Hotel Colorado in Glenwood Springs. Bryant remained horizontal in the back seat, his head covered in a towel, for the five-minute trip. The driver was told to keep the interior lights off.

As his companions handled the registration at the hotel, Bryant slipped in through a back door. It was 4:15 a.m. While Bryant was getting settled, O'Brien returned with one of the bodyguards, Michael Ortiz, to Cordillera to claim the athlete's luggage and belongings.

At 5:45 a.m., O'Brien returned Ortiz to the Hotel Colorado. The total fare came to $372, and in a strange show of bravado, Ortiz refused to tip O'Brien, all the while admonishing the driver that, "I wouldn't be telling anyone about this if I were you."

At 9:11 a.m. the morning of July 2, the Hotel and Spa at Cordillera billed Bryant $50 for a manicure appointment he did not keep. While Bryant was at the Colorado Hotel, an agreement was reached between Eagle County District Attorney Mark Hurlbert and the athlete's attorneys. No action was to be taken until July 7, in deference to the upcoming holiday weekend.

Informed of that agreement, Eagle County Sheriff Joe Hoy asked Clear Creek County Judge Russell Granger for an arrest warrant identifying Kobe Bean Bryant. Granger determined that there was probable cause that a sexual assault had been committed and there were reasonable grounds that Bryant had been the offending party. The warrant included one count of sexual assault, a Class Three felony, and one count of false imprisonment, based on Lilly's statement that Bryant had blocked her from leaving Room 35.

Hoy's action would take the shape of a slap at Hurlbert, since the district attorney ordinarily was the one to seek an arrest warrant. This fueled speculation in Los Angeles, in the Bryant camp, that the sheriff was an attention-seeking rube, in over his head. What Bryant's people didn't know was that Eagle County's top-cop didn't know who Kobe Bryant was, and apparently didn't care. When a deputy told Hoy about Bryant, the sheriff shrugged and looked at him with a puzzled expression. The deputy had to dribble an imaginary basketball and said, "You know, basketball?" Hoy, who seemed suspicious that Bryant was receiving special treatment because of his celebrity status, became annoyed. It wasn't long before he went directly to a judge and obtained the warrant.

At 7:15 a.m., his famous head spinning from a series of intrusions into a private world he'd protected with near fanaticism, Kobe Bryant checked out of the Hotel Colorado. The flight back home to Southern California would not be among the more comfortable in a life of privilege and achievement that suddenly was reeling out of control.

How would Bryant, who always learned from his mistakes and turned them to his advantage, find any redeeming value in this mess? The challenge of his life was now in front of him.

# 3

## STRUCK AT THE CORE

The dream life Kobe Bryant had constructed for himself, his young wife Vanessa and baby daughter Natalia in their Newport Beach fortress, was rapidly deteriorating into a nightmare. Nothing in his 24 charmed years on two continents had prepared him for the forces suddenly aligned against him.

Angst and anxiety were already his constant companions by the time the phone rang in his mansion on July 3. Eagle County Sheriff Joe Hoy had called Pamela Mackey, Bryant's lead attorney, informing her that Bryant was to return immediately to Colorado. The deal Mackey had struck with District Attorney Mark Hurlbert calling for Bryant to turn himself in on July 7 was no longer in effect. On the Fourth of July—Independence Day—Kobe Bryant would be booked on charges of sexual assault.

How does a man explain something like this to the woman who'd given him the most precious of gifts, a baby daughter, just six months earlier? How does a man tell his wife he cheated on her? How does he explain that their lives are about to implode because of his awful judgment?

Not easily.

This was a horror show that made the three airballs he'd shot as an 18-year-old Laker rookie, ending the playoff season for his team in Utah, seem like a picnic in the park. He couldn't go to the gym and fix this the way he did his jump shot. This wasn't going away.

Vanessa, still new to the stresses of motherhood at 21, became extremely upset when Kobe Bryant presented her with the staggering news. He'd told her just 24 hours before he returned to Eagle County to face the charges of sexual assault. At first she just gave him a sickly stare. Then her beautiful face soured and she broke down. Bryant called 911. When the dispatcher answered, he became uneasy and hung up. Bryant walked over to Vanessa who was visibly shaken, and kept telling her that he was sorry. Then the phone rang and Bryant answered it. It was the 911 operator asking if everything was all right.

Bryant explained that his wife needed medical attention and police, firefighters and paramedics soon swarmed the Bryant residence. Vanessa was treated for a medical condition, not an injury, and remained in the home.

This wasn't the first time Bryant's bride had to endure bad news. Three months earlier, on March 5, the slender, brown-eyed beauty had learned that her husband had discussed the possibility of divorce with a Los Angeles attorney, according to *Newsweek's* Allison Samuels. Upon hearing the news, she became panicked. Bryant, who didn't know how to calm her, assured her that everything would be all right. Rob Pelinka, a personal agent for Bryant who had become a close personal friend of the couple, rushed over to help and ended up calling 911. Hoag Memorial Hospital in Newport Beach later confirmed that an "adult woman" was taken to the hospital and placed on advanced life support.

Paramedics who treated Bryant's wife reported there was no evidence of a crime.

Now Bryant would need the support of his wife more than ever. Not only would she be invaluable in the court of public opinion, her love and loyalty would be priceless to him. Soon, the tables would be turned and it would be Bryant who feared divorce.

But it didn't take long for the media to descend on the biggest sports celebrity case since O.J. Simpson had dominated the airwaves. References to Simpson were unavoidable and unrelenting in the early stages. Like O.J., Kobe had transcended race to emerge as a beloved national figure, a familiar household name known as the face and voice for a wide array of products. The heavyweights—McDonalds, Coca-Cola and most recently Nike—had linked up with Bryant and "Kobe" was on his way to succeeding "Michael" off the court as well as on.

Like Jordan—and Simpson, prior to the summer of 1994—Bryant's image was pristine. He was the quintessential "good guy."

Days after word of his arrest broke, Bryant and Vanessa attended the ESPYs, an awards show in Los Angeles hosted by ESPN. He was shown by the cameras smiling broadly alongside his beautiful wife. Then came the Teen Choice Awards, again in L.A., where Bryant was honored as "favorite teen athlete," a distinction that brought howls from comics and critics alike, for obvious reasons.

Bryant showed up at the ceremony sporting a Muhammad Ali T-shirt and quoting Martin Luther King, Jr. It was a curious show of defiance that elicited support from the African-American community.

While Bryant was accepting his award, a 19-year-old woman a time zone away was dealing with notoriety of an entirely different kind.

Later, it was reported by *Newsweek* that Bryant's lawyer, Pamela Mackey, was infuriated when she learned that

Bryant had attended the award ceremony. Mackey felt that under the circumstances, Bryant's accepting the award would be perceived by the press as blatant disrespect for his situation.

When Mackey saw Bryant on television, she immediately called his bodyguards to "retrieve him." Mackey chastised Bryant for his defiance of her and warned him that if he disobeyed her again, he would have to seek counsel elsewhere.

Then there was The Ring.

The moment he had arrived in Los Angeles as a fresh-faced rookie straight out of Lower Merion High School in suburban Philadelphia, Bryant had spoken of his desire to win NBA championships—plural.

"The ring's the thing," was his mantra.

Along with Shaquille O'Neal and a solid supporting cast, Bryant, tougher than the rest under pressure, made his dream a reality in 2000 for new coach Phil Jackson, and won two more titles. A month after the quest for a fourth straight title was crushed by eventual champion San Antonio, Bryant found himself in the market for a ring not officially endorsed by the NBA.

In what was widely perceived as an effort to purchase his wife's support, Bryant bought a $4 million diamond-encrusted ring in Santa Monica. Once again, he was the butt of jokes from masters Leno and Letterman and countless lesser talents.

It was lonely inside the walls of his Newport Beach mansion. Bryant never had much time for social relationships, but now his universe was limited to Vanessa and his bodyguards.

He had always cut off any and all attempts to enter his private world. Over the years several writers were forced to cancel magazine cover stories when Bryant refused to cooperate. Even his marriage to Vanessa Laine, in the spring of 2001, was veiled in secrecy. Bryant tried to keep the whole thing under wraps and was upset with reporters when they inquired about it. He was unwilling to accept that people wanted to know about his private life.

But on June 30, thanks to a private act that became all too public, Bryant was now a public figure in ways he'd never imagined, his every move now instantly placed under a media microscope he'd fought to hide from over the past five years.

In the past, Bryant had been able to dig deep and find the inner resources to make everything right. This was his M.O., his calling card. He was tougher than the rest, and he knew it right from the start.

He was also more charming than the rest, something Southern California reporters discovered when they met him for the first time, a month shy of his 18th birthday, at the L. A. Lakers' pre-Staples Center home, the fabulous Forum in suburban Inglewood.

It was the summer of 1996. Sports scribes, many of them jaded veterans not easily impressed, saw something different about this kid—his easy, confident manner; his reverence for the great players of the past; the way he looked you in the eyes when he spoke with you. Those things endeared him instantly to the grizzled crew of L.A. sports columnists. It was love at first sight.

Over the years, from his fitful start as the man-child in the company of superstar center Shaquille O'Neal, through three scintillating championship runs starting in the spring of 2000, Bryant was the sports columnists' favorite athlete. In tiffs with coaches (Del Harris and Phil Jackson) and teammates (Shaq, most prominently) the columnists unfailingly went to print aligned with Bryant, scolding his elders for not cutting him some slack, for not realizing that he was a kid in a man's world trying to find his way, seeking his identity.

The writers admired Bryant's mind-blowing physical gifts, but it was much more than dunks and knee-busting crossover moves. It was the way the young man handled himself in hard times that hooked the old men (and a few women) with the notepad. Kobe never ran and hid. Unlike Shaq, who would often disappear after a loss, Kobe was always there, at his locker, honest and forthright, telling it like it was.

Bryant took many of the reporters back to the days of Magic Johnson, Kareem Abdul-Jabbar and friends. Kobe exuded the spirit of what it was like to play because he loved the game and because he wanted to win.

Along with Bryant's dad Joe, Earvin "Magic" Johnson had been Kobe's hero as a kid. (In fact, their styles were similar in many respects, which was ironic since it seemed as though the trademark "assist" that made Magic so beloved was clearly lacking from the younger Bryant's repertoire). But Bryant did indeed have some Magic in him—the engaging smile and manner, the ability to break down a game, the willingness to hold court with the media and impart insight until it was time to go home and start thinking about the next game.

"I'm all about basketball," he'd say, and they believed him. Magic had been just like that as a young player, before dizzying stardom in the chic-capital of the universe turned his head.

About the game, Kobe Bryant was amazingly mature. Beyond that, it was hard to know what he was like. He was a private person from the start, and the media respected that.

His good-guy traits soon lifted Bryant into Magic's realm as a personality, making him the most popular of the Lakers outside the dressing room—and eventually the most popular player in the league, judging by jersey sales.

Cynics would look in the rearview mirror after "the incident" and see all of that as a calculated power play, carefully designed by family and agents. Many die-hard scribes preferred to think that it was simply a great, young athlete in love with the game and his life—being himself, doing what came naturally. There didn't seem to be an ounce of pretense in Bryant as he lifted his game with a total command found only in the greatest of players.

That first day, at the Forum, columnists wrote of how this was love at first sight for the Lakers' management as well as for the assembled media. Kobe Bryant had that kind of instant impact, giving a sense that here was a special young man.

Seven summers after that first meeting, almost to the day that Bryant arrived at the Lakers practice holding court with the press, the news flashed across the television screen: Kobe Bryant arrested. Those same columnists who had so easily embraced Kobe Bryant were now forced to scramble and rack their brains for some clue as to what had happened. Kobe Bryant was now in the game of his life.

# 4

## THE HEART OF A CHAMPION

The news was earth shattering.

Nike, the company that made Michael Jordan and Tiger Woods rich and famous beyond imagination, made a bold statement before the 2003 NBA draft when it announced an astonishing $90 million deal with LeBron James, the Ohio high school phenom. The huge investment signaled that the sneaker and apparel powerhouse was convinced that James was the future of the NBA, that he was the man who would carry the swoosh banner for years to come.

At the same time, Nike was negotiating a deal with Kobe Bryant. It had to be bewildering to the more established Bryant that James was suddenly the chosen one.

In terms of achievement, there was no comparison between James and Bryant. The Lakers' soaring guard had won three championships, emerged as an all-league first team performer and was immensely popular across the board with all demographics—his jersey the leading seller in the league for the 2002-03 season.

What Nike was telling him, without coming right out and saying it, was that Bryant didn't have the "street cred" among the urban youth that made James so appealing. This became apparent when Nike announced its deal with Kobe amounting to about $45 million—not bad, of course, but only half the amount awarded the unproven teen who had not yet even been drafted.

According to industry experts, Bryant was seen as too upscale, too slick and not edgy enough to carry the street appeal of young King James. Kobe didn't favor tattoos or bling-bling, going with an old-school look throughout his seven seasons in the league. Inner-city kids, people in the know concluded, preferred the sneakers of lesser performers with less polish and more neon.

Bryant was viewed as the counter to Allen Iverson, the hugely popular Philadelphia 76ers star who sported cornrows and pounds of jewelry and was known to get into trouble with the law on occasion. Never comfortable with Iverson and his image, the NBA was delighted to endorse Bryant as its future centerpiece, filling the void left by Michael Jordan.

But when word surfaced of the young James's great fortune, it had to rankle Bryant. What had LeBron done to warrant such royal treatment besides dominate high school kids, something Kobe had done eight years earlier in suburban Pennsylvania? Bryant, in contrast to Iverson and a number of other young NBA stars, was squeaky clean, the classic All-American kid next door. Kobe was seen more frequently on TV commercials than any other contemporary NBA star, including his celebrated teammate, Shaquille O'Neal. That never sat particularly well with Shaq, but at least O'Neal's salary from the Lakers continued to dwarf Bryant's, giving the giant center the satisfaction that his employers realized who was more valuable. With the heavyweights of the endorsement industry, from McDonald's to Coca-Cola (with its Sprite ads) to Spalding, Kobe was seen as solid gold, a dream salesman. He had a cool, easy manner and a suave charm that reminded everyone of His Airness at his commercial peak.

Even without premium street cred, Bryant was on his way to challenging the master of space and time, Jordan, not only on the court but in the endorsement world, which Michael had ruled for close to two decades.

At least that was the universal impression before the events of June 30, 2003, would alter perceptions forever with respect to the Laker superstar.

Kobe Bryant arrested on a felony count of sexual assault. News does not come much more stunning than that. Where did he go wrong? How had Mr. Perfect taken such an unbelievable fall in a remote Colorado town?

Perhaps one of the keys lay with Jerry West, Bryant's mentor, the man who brought him to L.A. from a Pennsylvania high school campus. Kobe was like a son to West, who left L.A. in 2002 and moved far off to develop the fledgling Memphis Grizzlies. "Mr. Clutch," West was always at his best under pressure, and he was someone Bryant would ordinarily need close by during troubling times.

Now, with West in Tennessee, who among the Lakers' personnel would Bryant turn to for counsel? Magic Johnson certainly was available. A minority share holder in the franchise he had led the team to five championships during the "Showtime" era of the 1980s. Johnson had been through it all, rebuilding his own tattered reputation after his revelations of misguided sexual adventures in the wake of his positive HIV test in November 1991. Magic, tirelessly reaching out in the community, built a business empire and established himself as a force for change across the country with a wide range of businesses in inner cities. Bryant surely could benefit from Magic's background, his experience in dealing with adversity, if he chose to reach out and touch the Hall of Famer.

Like Johnson, Bryant had displayed a remarkable resilience over his years as a Laker. There were charges of selfish play, misunderstandings with coaches, the long-running, headline-stealing feud with O'Neal. It was a series of storms for Bryant in his life by the Pacific Ocean. Committed to his craft, dedicated to making himself the greatest player ever, Kobe rose above those obstacles to become a champion and a leader.

But this business in Colorado, these charges of sexual misconduct with a 19-year-old concierge, this was something different. This was a brand of trouble Bryant never could have imagined confronting during his rise to stardom. It was at this time that Bryant needed his friends to stand up and say, "I know Kobe Bryant, and Kobe Bryant wouldn't do this." But these people did not surface when the news from Colorado broke.

One of the problems with Bryant was that he'd been so difficult to get to know, not only with media types searching for insights into what made him tick, but also with teammates and coaches. Some insiders volunteered the opinion that Kobe had inherited his father's mistrust of the outside world.

Joe "Jellybean" Bryant had been a talented forward in the Magic Johnson mold during the '70s, but he never achieved the brand of stardom that would define his son. Joe was viewed as a journeyman, a role player, and he privately burned to be the main man in the fashion of his Philadelphia teammate, Julius Erving. Only when he moved to Europe, far removed from his native land, did Joe Bryant find that kind of professional success.

It was while his dad was starring in Italy that Kobe began to develop his own style. In his professional life, Kobe was expansive about the game—he loved everything about it, including practice—but he was intensely protective of his private world. Questions about his private life with wife Vanessa and their daughter, Natalia, born in January 2003, were met with icy stares and routinely rejected. Reporters covering the Lakers quickly learned what was off limits with Bryant, and it was pretty much everything not associated with the game of basketball.

Bryant was born with complete faith in his exceptional talents, his competitive drive carrying him even when seemingly everybody else, coaches and teammates included, openly doubted him. He always prevailed, too, by sheer force of will if necessary.

Flashback: Game 7, 2000 Western Conference finals, Lakers down by 15 in the fourth quarter against Portland. Who was the man who took charge, who brought the team all the way back with a raging fury, who tossed that gorgeously symbolic lob to Shaquille O'Neal for the slam dunk that brought the Staples Center house—and the Trail Blazers—down?

Kobe Bryant, of course.

The kid was 21 that magical Sunday in L.A. When older teammates were wilting and fading, ready to surrender, he soared and roared. Kobe visibly loved pressure, lived for the moment. Here was the rarest kind of athlete, the one who instinctively raised his game right along with the stakes. Say what you will about his attitude, his arrogance, his ego. When everything was on the line, this was the guy you wanted with the ball if you were Phil Jackson and coaching the Lakers. Bryant was every rival coach's nightmare.

"He has that fierceness of Michael Jordan," San Antonio coach Gregg Popovich said, having just watched a soaring Kobe Bryant destroy his Spurs in the 2001 Western Conference finals. "He wants to put his foot on your throat."

As with everything else in what had once been Bryant's perfectly ordered world, those graphic words took twisted new meaning in the wake of the events of June 30.

From the time he arrived in the NBA in the fall of 1996, joining the talent-rich Lakers as a prodigy from Lower Merion High School in suburban Philly, Bryant had a personal mission. He burned not to be like Mike, as the popular Nike ads of the day urged America's youthful dreamers. Bryant was determined to be greater than Jordan, greater even than his boyhood hero, Magic Johnson.

Kobe Bryant was plotting a course that he believed would certify him as the best ever to play the game.

Orders don't come much taller, but Bryant, 6-foot-7 and deceptively strong, never was one to back down from a challenge. A young man who was willing to physically fight a behemoth outweighing him by more than one hundred pounds—Shaq Diesel himself—during a scrimmage early in his Laker career, Bryant was not readily intimidated.

Growing up in Italy Kobe had learned to live inside his head. There wasn't much in the way of hoop competition during those formative years from age 6 to 12, before he would return to America. Left basically to his own devices, Bryant became solitary in his pursuits—a trait that would remain dominant as he grew into a phenomenal high school talent in suburban Philadelphia.

No teen his size had ever made it big coming into the NBA straight from high school. Only bigger men like Moses Malone, and then a year before Kobe, Kevin Garnett—had made a splash leaving the senior prom for the big time. Bryant, whose prom date was the popular singer/actress Brandy (on the advice of his handlers he had left his actual girlfriend of several years at home as he squired the headline-generating songstress around town), was maneuvered into the Lakers' hands by some shrewd deal-making brokered by the legendary Jerry West. In the space of eight days in the summer of '96, West put together the foundation for a future dynasty, landing Kobe and Shaq, who signed as a free agent.

West believed in Bryant when few others did, stealing him from the Charlotte Hornets in one of the most lopsided trades in NBA history. It didn't look that way at the time, given that Bryant lasted until the 13th pick in the draft. He was seen as too frail, too fragile and too selfish to make much of an immediate or permanent impact.

What others couldn't see—what West grasped during Kobe's eye-popping workout before the draft—was that he had the heart of a champion.

Those first few seasons would have buckled weaker athletes. Bryant, too young to know better, thought talent would be enough to make him an overnight success. But resistance arrived in a variety of forms, from coaches (Del Harris, initially) who felt he needed seasoning, to teammates (notably Shaq) who believed Bryant needed to be cut down to size. Rookies shouldn't walk into the NBA expecting to be handed everything, was the prevailing opinion.

When Kobe's one friend early in his career, Eddie Jones, was traded to Charlotte for Glen Rice during the 1999 season, Bryant truly was a man apart.

Teammates had little idea what to think of the kid who kept to himself, his life seemingly limited to room service and video games. Derek Fisher, who came into the NBA with Bryant and shared the backcourt with him, admitted he didn't have a real personal conversation with Kobe until they'd been in the league for several seasons.

Hardened veterans of the circuit didn't appreciate it when Bryant would openly criticize them for hanging out in clubs and living the high life. He hadn't paid enough dues to be making judgments like that, and they let him know how they felt, driving a further wedge in a relationship that for practical purposes didn't even exist off the court.

"Who know where he go?" wily backcourt partner Ron Harper once said of Bryant. "Who know what he do?" And this was one of the Lakers whom Bryant privately respected.

It was in his fifth season, after he'd won an NBA title and was on his way to another, that Bryant began surfacing occasionally at the clubs, accompanied by his bodyguards. He was now 21.

By now, the company Kobe enjoyed was the most exclusive imaginable: legends of the game, best-ever names such as Michael and Magic, West and Oscar Robertson. These became his historical reference points when playoff frustration gave way to championship banners and parades.

The catalyst in the transformation was the celebrated Chicago Zen master, Phil Jackson. With his eccentric manner and maverick ways, Jackson managed to stitch together all these disparate parts and achieve instant success with a 1999-00 title run cresting with that Game 7 comeback against Portland, one of the most dramatic in league history.

That was largely Kobe's doing, and not even his loudest critics could deny it. His coming-out party as a superstar was validated in the finals, against Indiana's Pacers. When Shaq fouled out late in Game 4 at Indiana, Kobe carried his team to an overtime triumph by dominating the five-minute extra session.

A legend was born. Bryant now stood apart in every respect.

There would be two more championships in succession, but not without strife and struggle. Shaq and Kobe squared off for control of the ball and the team during a fitful 2000-01 season, creating an internal storm that threatened the dynasty's foundation.

Jackson did little to intervene, suggesting that these things had to be worked out by the principals themselves. Jackson's sage assistant, Tex Winter, offered this assessment of the Star Wars: "Super players have super egos. They wouldn't be here if they didn't. They take challenges, sometimes with a teammate. It's the nature of the beast."

To the relief of everyone in Lakerdom, Kobe and Shaq smoothed out their differences and the Lakers stormed through the conference playoffs without a loss, sweeping Phoenix, Sacramento and San Antonio in an awesome display. The lone post-season loss came in Game 1 of the finals against Philadelphia and Allen Iverson.

That was a duel the NBA and network officials craved: "The Answer," Iverson, with his outlaw image, vs. Kobe, the clean-cut anti-Iverson.

It was no contest. Kobe and Co. blew away Iverson's Sixers to win the title in five.

The three-peat in 2001-02 did not come without turmoil and tribulation. The one constant was Bryant, playing at a supremely high level all season, lifting his team past San Antonio and Sacramento, then sweeping New Jersey in the finals. All doubts had been swept aside, along with the Nets. Only the few surviving Kobe haters would try to deny that this was the best all-around talent in the game.

Former rival Shaq made that rather startling admission himself during the 2001 playoffs when he labeled Kobe "the best player in the league, by far . . . the best on all nine planets." Veteran power forward Horace Grant, a cog in Chicago's dynastic machinery in the '90s, predicted that Shaq and Kobe wouldn't stop until they'd won eight or nine championships.

Only Bill Russell and Magic Johnson had enjoyed Bryant's championship profile by age 24. Kobe had claimed three NBA titles—one more than Wilt Chamberlain, Philadelphia's storied superhero—while routinely securing dramatic playoff victories with late-game heroics. He'd played in five All-Star games and was named MVP of the showcase in his hometown of Philly. He was slam-dunk champion and all-league first team twice.

Here was a total force approaching Jordan's class, with Magic's rare ability to raise teammates' level of play with superior passing skills. Even Jordan's good pal, Charles Barkley, admitted that Bryant was more advanced at his age than Michael had been.

Kobe was, as Laker announcer Stu Lantz liked to call him, "The Package." He had all the goods.

Off the court, Bryant also was steam-rolling into Jordan's realm, establishing himself as the endorsement king of his generation. With Nike having jumped on board the Bryant train, mega-millions awaited him in future deals with the heavyweights of industry.

His private life was always declared off limits, leaving the media to speculate about how happy he was away from the arena lights. All efforts to acquire insight into this celebrity's inner world were met with, at best, blank stares from Bryant. When one writer asked if he'd mind revealing the content of some of his poetry for a profile, Bryant slam-dunked the idea instantly. "Nobody's going to read my poetry," he said, stalking off.

Yet, in the workplace, he was cooperative, available and unfailingly polite. Unlike stormy O'Neal, the Lakers' temperamental superstar, Bryant was a cool breeze. He could be counted on to give reasoned responses to questions pertaining to the game and his team.

Around the league, Kobe was emerging with the same exalted, impeccable standing once reserved for Julius Erving, Jordan and Johnson, the suave, silver-tongued superstars who paved the way for this incredibly wealthy new generation. Unlike many peers, Bryant—raised by a father who'd played alongside Dr. J in Philly—fully appreciated the efforts of those who had gone before him. The afro Kobe sprouted early in his career was an expressive throwback to the '70s, sparking a new fashion trend not just in the league but in America's inner cities as well.

Kobe's influence was expanding into rare Air indeed.

As open as he could be with his basketball views, Bryant's private life was a book that remained shut tight. What was known about Kobe and Vanessa Laine was that they met in 1999 when he was 21 and she was 16. She was appearing in a Snoop Dogg video, and he happened to be in the studio working on a rap CD that was never completed. Bryant was instantly smitten by the Latin beauty.

A high school student at the time, Vanessa shared Kobe's interest, and they were soon an item. The romance became big news in spite of Bryant's vigilance, and it eventually wore on Kobe's parents. Joe and Pam Bryant had been an everyday presence in Kobe's life, but that changed as Vanessa moved in, first figuratively, then literally.

The Bryants, who had lived with Kobe in coastal Pacific Palisades early in his Laker career, relocated to Philadelphia, their influence on their son diminishing in direct proportion to Vanessa's expanding role.

Bryant had never experienced such complexities in his personal life. Early in his relationship with Vanessa, he'd been pressured to make a decision. Vanessa was only 17 when they became seriously involved, and it was clear that if Kobe didn't step up and prove his loyalty to her, her family would not take it lightly.

Rumors surfaced that officials at Marina High School in Huntington Beach were considering complaining to legal authorities about the relationship. They reportedly didn't approve of the attention caused by one of their students wearing expensive diamond rings and getting dropped off in the morning by a pro basketball player five years her senior. All of this was heady stuff for Vanessa, raised in a Catholic family.

Before long, Bryant moved Vanessa in with him in Pacific Palisades and they began house hunting in Orange County, closer to her family. The couple was wed in April of 2001 in a highly private ceremony with none of his teammates in attendance, though Shaq and Co. shouldn't have felt overlooked; Joe and Pam Bryant weren't there.

Finding the home of their dreams in exclusive Newport Beach, the Bryants settled in and launched what appeared to be a happy life together. Natalia arrived in January 2003, and she was clearly the light of Kobe's life.

If ever there appeared to be a perfect world inhabited by a dream athlete, this was it. The scrapes he'd endured early in his career with Shaq and coaches appeared to be yesterday's news for this blemish-free superstar.

And now, out of the blue, good-guy Kobe Bryant, the NBA's crown prince, was charged with felony sexual assault. An athlete with few equals was suddenly facing the adversary of his life in the form of the criminal justice system. A performer who lived to control situations would be leaving his fate in the hands of others, notably an aggressive defense team captained by Pamela Mackey.

Suddenly, in a life turned upside down, Bryant's surpassing virtues as an athlete were seen in an entirely different, disturbing light. Assets became liabilities, his every motive and motivation were debated. His celebrated commitment to greatness took the shape of raw obsession, inviting questions at every turn.

Known as old school in part because he resisted the tide of body art and flashy jewelry, Bryant showed up two months after being charged with rape bearing one tattoo for his daughter, another for his wife.

All of his perceived strengths turned into weaknesses in the time it took him to open a door to his suite and invite in a 19-year-old concierge.

That single-minded purpose, that insatiable drive of Bryant's to be the best of all time on the basketball court was now viewed by critics as evidence of stunted emotional growth.

That sense of detachment, that need to be left alone to his own devices in order to maximize his astonishing gifts was seen as a sign of arrested development, of an inability to blend into his environment in a normal manner.

That refusal to surrender under the most dire of game circumstances, that extraordinary ability to elevate his performance almost on command. That surfaced in some minds as the dark will of someone who can't take no for an answer.

All of those qualities that made him a superstar beyond his own wildest imaginings had come back to haunt Bryant. He was innocent until proven guilty in the court of law, but in the court of public opinion, his image had taken a battering that would require much more than a "not guilty" verdict to heal.

# 5

## SPIN CITIES

Fame finds some people, whether they want it or not. So it was with Mark Hurlbert. One day he was an upwardly mobile district attorney making $67,000 a year, appointed by the governor to serve as the DA of Eagle County, Colorado. The next day the whole world was watching his every move, hanging on his every syllable.

Unlike Kobe Bryant, Hurlbert wasn't used to being in the national spotlight, and unlike Bryant, he didn't have the misfortune of seeing his heroic image begin to fade in a cloud of suspicion.

At 3 p.m. on the Friday afternoon of October 18, Hurlbert stepped into the sunshine outside the Eagle County Justice Center, peered into a battery of cameras and microphones recording the moment for an international audience, and made the statement that would resonate from Los Angeles to Tokyo.

"We have charged Kobe Bean Bryant with sexual assault, a Class Three felony," Hurlbert said. He then detailed the potential sentences: probation or four years to life in prison. A fine—the very least of Bryant's concerns—could range from $3,000 to $750,000.

Life in prison? For Kobe Bryant? The possibility caused global shock waves.

In a heartbeat, a time zone away, the forces aligned by a multimillion-dollar athlete, a franchise player if ever there was one, leapt to the task, preparing a quick and dramatic response designed to overwhelm the impact of Hurlbert's announcement. This would be a case study in crisis management.

Just three hours after Hurlbert dropped his bomb, Bryant, accompanied by his wife, would sit behind a microphone at Staples Center, his home court in Los Angeles. The beloved basketball star would emotionally admit to having committed adultery while vehemently denying that he forced himself on the 19-year-old woman—a necessary component to the felony charge.

Hollywood screenwriters couldn't have produced anything more spellbinding. It was the classic David vs. Goliath confrontation: diminutive Eagle County, with its rural population and limited resources, matched against the great Kobe Bryant and his team of high-priced, high-powered lawyers and investigators.

Hurlbert had taken two and a half weeks to make his decision, studying every piece of evidence and every conceivable angle while leaning on the counsel of fellow prosecutors from across the state. *The People of the State of Colorado Against Kobe Bean Bryant*—case number 03CR204—was approached with an understanding of the enormity of the challenge. In a matter of hours after Hurlbert's carefully planned announcement, Bryant and his lawyers would retaliate.

"As in any sex-assault case, ladies and gentlemen, this did not come easily," Hurlbert said, taking questions from reporters among the several hundred people assembled at the steps of the justice center. "With any felony, it's a difficult decision—and I take it seriously.

"I have an ethical burden not to prosecute unless I can prove my case beyond a reasonable doubt. I believe I can prove it beyond a reasonable doubt."

In the court document, Hurlbert stated that "Kobe Bean Bryant unlawfully, feloniously and knowingly inflicted sexual intrusion or sexual penetration on [the victim], causing submission of the victim . . . through the application of physical force or physical violence."

Hurlbert, who grew up in neighboring Summit County and attended Dartmouth and the University of Colorado Law School, had prosecuted high profile cases before. But this was another league altogether. This would have a global audience, the lights and cameras invading his every waking hour for the foreseeable future.

"We're going to treat this like any other sexual assault case," Hurlbert said, "even though I'm saying that while I'm looking at 20 television cameras. In any case, you look at everything: physical evidence, testimony, everything.

"Any sexual assault case is difficult. The overriding goal is justice."

There was, in the Bryant matter, a weight of material to be considered. There would be no infamous glove to be analyzed, as in the O.J. Simpson murder trial that gripped the nation a decade earlier.

"It's the totality of the case, not one piece of evidence in particular," Hurlbert said. "Ninety percent of sexual assault cases are like that."

Hurlbert moved to dispel the notion that the trial would have to be moved to another venue.

"The crime occurred in Eagle County," he said, "and the people of Eagle County have a right to hear it."

Hurlbert would admit that nothing in his experience had prepared him for the magnitude of the moment, or for confronting aggressive big-city journalists from around the country.

"Dealing with the local press became something I realized was a part of the job. Dealing with the national press . . . that's something else."

Sensing a media onslaught that could make the alleged victim's life unbearable, Hurlbert asked that her privacy be maintained.

"It has been difficult for her," he said, "and she will not talk to the media."

In Los Angeles, meanwhile, Bryant's team, captained by the assertive Mackey, was all set to do some serious talking. But first, through attorneys Mackey and Harold Haddon, the Bryants issued statements.

From Kobe Bryant: "I am innocent of the charges filed today. I did not assault the woman who is accusing me. I made the mistake of adultery. I have to answer to my wife and my God for my actions that night, and I pray that both will forgive me.

"Nothing that happened June 30 was against the will of the woman who now falsely accuses me.

"These false allegations have hurt my family. I will fight against these allegations with all my strength. My wife is the strongest person I know. She is willing to stand by me despite my mistake. That means everything to me.

"I have so much to live for. And by that I do not mean the contracts, or the money, or the fame. I mean my family. I will fight for them.

"I appreciate all those who have supported me. Thank you for believing in me. My family and I are going to need your support and prayers now more than ever."

From Vanessa Bryant: "I know that my husband has made a mistake—the mistake of adultery. He and I will have to deal with that within our marriage, and we will do so. He is not a criminal.

"I know that he did not commit a crime; he did not assault anyone. He is a loving and kind husband and father. I believe in his innocence.

"Because I know him to be innocent, I will stand by him and we will face this together. I will give him all the strength and support he needs to face these false accusations. I will not let him face these accusations alone.

"I know Kobe better than anyone. The great person you see on the court and in the public is a far greater person off the court."

While Team Bryant was getting ready to launch its counterattack from Staples Center, Eagle County Sheriff Joe Hoy was explaining that his decision to seek a bench warrant, a task normally reserved for the district attorney, was a simple miscommunication.

"I am confident that Mark Hurlbert and the people in his office have made the appropriate decision," Hoy said. "We're pleased with what the district attorney did, but that doesn't mean we're celebrating. Who wants this? No one wants this."

Hoy described the teenage concierge and her family as "standing tall" through the ordeal, adding, "I think I understand she's in for a rough ride. The investigators indicated something like this could be tough."

Hoy hailed the announcement by Hurlbert as testimony to "our effective system of law enforcement. I am proud that the people in this Sheriff's Office have carried out their responsibility professionally, reflecting their many years of experience."

In Los Angeles, meanwhile, Lakers management was attempting to produce an appropriate response to an impossible situation.

"Naturally, we're disappointed with today's announcement," said the team's general manager, Mitch Kupchak, a former NBA star.

"While there are many questions concerning this issue, we will wait for time and the judicial process to answer them.

In the meantime, we will continue to offer our support to Kobe and his family."

NBA Commissioner David Stern offered no immediate comment, and, apart from a Maverick owner in Dallas named Mark Cuban, that would set the tone throughout the league. Cuban would soon set off a media firestorm by declaring that the fascination with the Bryant case would be good for business, drawing casual fans to the sport. If it was a dubious position, one at least had to admire Cuban for his candor in a sea of "no comment."

Now the stage was set, literally, for Bryant to respond to the charges filed in Colorado. Wearing blue jeans and a white sweater, he emerged expressionless from behind a partition, joined by his lead attorney and his wife. There was a distinct feminine cast to the press conference, a point that would be observed in the aftermath by media consultants who enthusiastically applauded the performance.

Mackey came on strong as she unflinchingly declared her client's innocence, claiming the sexual encounter was "between two consenting adults."

Turning it over to Bryant, Mackey watched as he took a few gulps, gathered his thoughts and formed difficult words, his hand entwined with Vanessa's throughout.

"I didn't force her to do anything against her will," Bryant said. "I'm innocent. I'm sitting here in front of you guys furious at myself—disgusted at myself—for making a mistake . . . of adultery. I love my wife with all my heart. She is my backbone."

Gazing at Vanessa, mother of his six-month-old daughter, Bryant tried to verbalize that love: "You're a blessing. You're a piece of my heart, the air I breathe. And you're the strongest person I know. I'm so sorry for having to put you through this, putting my family through this."

"I'm like everyone else. I mourn. I cry. I sit before you today embarrassed and ashamed for committing adultery. If I could turn back the hands of time . . . ."

As if dazed that this actually could be happening to him, Bryant paused, then added: "I'm innocent."

He kept shaking his head while trying in vain to moisten his parched lips. Vanessa, who sat silently, seemed in a daze of her own. Motionless, with the exception of gently moving fingers across her husbands clasped hands, Vanessa Laine Bryant, who had been revered by her husband, his friends and boys from her childhood, faced the strangely foreign feeling of having been passed over for another woman.

"I have a lot at stake," Bryant said, "and it has nothing to do with the game of basketball and it has nothing to do with endorsements. It has nothing to do with that. It has to do with my family—and being falsely accused.

"This is about us. This is about our family. Shoulder to shoulder, we are going to fight this all the way to the end."

For his legions of fans, this had to be almost as difficult to watch as it was for Bryant to deliver.

In his time in Los Angeles, Bryant had grown up before an adoring public, taking the long walk from irrepressible teen to mature and respected man. Prior to the sex assault charges, the NBA had been in the process of anointing Kobe the new Michael.

Now all of that had blown up and his world was rocked to its foundation. It would take years to accurately calculate the full extent of the damage. But right away, it was evident to those in the sports business field that Bryant had sustained blows to his stature and reputation that could not be repaired—ever.

"The image [of Bryant] was of a perfect role model, a superstar athlete who didn't have a parking ticket, the All-American boy," said Bob Williams, chief executive of Burns Sports & Celebrities Inc. in Evanston, Ill. "Now, well, that image is tarnished. Until the trial, his image is going to take a beating." Less than a year earlier, Williams' firm had sponsored a poll in which Bryant finished third among the most desired sports endorsers, trailing only Tiger Woods and Michael Jordan.

# 6

## THE BELIEVER

While Kobe Bryant was trying to get accustomed to his new private hell, Lilly Fuller was getting used to her own.

While the NBA athlete professed his innocence to nearly a hundred million viewers nationwide, the woman he allegedly raped watched him in silence.

As she sat quietly on a sofa between her two closest friends, Luke and Starlene Bray, she blanched and visibly shuddered as the camera zoomed in on Bryant sitting intently beside his lovely wife. A feeling of total emptiness came over Lilly, and for the first time she found herself looking into the eyes of the man whom she told the police had forced himself on her. A wave of fear swept through her, and she felt sick to her stomach. Then, almost instinctively, she turned her attention to Bryant's wife Vanessa, checking out her long, straight brown hair, her almost perfect complexion and her gentle, somewhat vacuous eyes.

She was surprised that a man who was married to such a beautiful woman would risk losing her, particularly to spend an evening with someone like herself. Lilly Fuller had never thought she was pretty. She had never understood why the boys who chased after her did so, and more than ever she was mystified as to why this superstar athlete who had everything to lose and nothing to gain risked it all just to spend a few minutes with her in a Colorado hotel room.

As she looked deeper into Vanessa's eyes, Lilly was filled with compassion. That empty, zoned look reminded her all too much of herself when she stared into the mirror. At that moment, Lilly realized that she and Vanessa Bryant were both undoubtedly suffering from some very similar symptoms as the nightmare rolled on. She realized that they would both endure a series of life transformations before the trial was over and a verdict was delivered to the court and to the American people.

But what concerned Lilly at the moment wasn't the verdict that would be rendered in the Eagle County Courthouse. She was worried about a court in a different jurisdiction whose rules were subject to those of the journalists, critics and tabloid headlines which shaped public opinion. She had felt strong and confident when Mark Hurlbert had appeared on national television and announced that he could successfully prosecute the case and get a conviction. But now, Kobe Bean Bryant, skilled athlete and Los Angeles Lakers champion, was employing the services of mastermind criminal defense lawyers and an entourage of public relations spin-doctors who were upstaging her heroic prosecutor. They were about to distract the national press from Hurlbert's statement by pointing to the sympathy and compassion that emanated from millions of Bryant's admirers and supporters.

It was dawning on Lilly that she hardly knew how incredibly popular and successful he *really* was. Now, it would be only a matter of time before he started using his fame and success to win public support. Men wanted to be

Bryant and women wanted to be with him. Would *anyone* really believe that she had told him no? *Anyone at all?*

As her best friends Luke and Starlene Bray sat next to her, Lilly recalled how she had first met them when she was just a child in Eagle. She'd befriended Starlene in grade school and the two were virtually inseparable until high school graduation, when she finally left to start college at the University of Northern Colorado. Lilly had often told her friend that she was like therapy for her, and whenever she suffered from heartbreak and disappointment in the past, Star was the one she would turn to.

Only a few short days before Bryant's team launched their retaliatory strike against Hurlbert, Starlene received a phone call from Andrea Beaumont, a producer at ABC's *Good Morning America*, asking her if she would like to speak to the nation on her friend's behalf. Starlene contemplated the offer and decided to ask Lilly if she would feel comfortable with it.

Lilly, who was well aware that public opinion had turned against her, told her friend, "Everyone already hates me anyway, so go ahead." Star called Beaumont back and accepted her offer.

After a dreary, sleepy flight, the Colorado friends landed at LaGuardia airport in Queens. They were soon in the midst of Manhattan skyscrapers and headed for the TV studio. Luke, who was mistrusting of big cities, wanted to get the interview over with and return to Colorado as soon as possible. Starlene, however, was happy to be back east. The last time she'd visited, she was 13 years old. Her family had traveled to New Jersey for a wedding and ended up visiting her aunt who was diagnosed with cancer. The aunt promised her niece the next time she was in town she would show her the Big Apple. One month later, her aunt died.

As Starlene was drifting back into childhood memories, the limousine dropped them at the Millennium Broadway

Hotel, where they underwent a brief pre-interview on the phone with an ABC producer. Afterwards, the couple had lunch at a nearby Italian restaurant with some members of the *Good Morning America* cast, who then walked with them to ABC's network headquarters.

Only Starlene would face the nation that day. Luke, who was more apprehensive about being seen on nation-wide television, waited inside a dark studio control room listening to other network shows simultaneously. Luke noticed that two of his friends were on with NBC's Katie Couric shortly before his own wife took the stage at ABC. While he carefully examined all the high-tech equipment in the studio, Luke heard a friend from Eagle use Lilly's real name on the air. Astonished, he looked up at the television screen while several technicians in the room gasped.

It was the first time anyone had said Lilly's name on the air, and he was annoyed by it. Luke didn't know about rape shield laws or the journalistic covenant of non-disclosure at the time, but his intuition told him that using the name of an alleged rape victim had to be illegal, and certainly not eth-ical. He knew that NBC's allowance of the name was likely a technical slip, but he was still concerned about it. He hoped that ABC was better prepared.

He still wasn't sure how he felt about talking to the press at all, but he understood his wife's decision to go on the air. While many of his friends were taking advantage of the opportunity to get luxurious treatment from the media, with-out having anything of true substance to say, Luke and his wife considered themselves to be in New York strictly on business. They didn't want to be wined and dined or taken to a Yankees game or Broadway show. They just wanted to talk about their friend to the press and go home. By the end of Starlene's interview, the couple was both pleased and satisfied that they had effectively spoken up for a friend in need.

# UPSET BY MEDIA REPORTS FRIEND SPEAKS UP FOR KOBE BRYANT'S ACCUSER

## ABC NEWS

E A G L E, Colo., July 14—*The young woman who accused basketball star Kobe Bryant is a "trustworthy, thoughtful" person now "in hiding" from the media, a friend of the 19-year-old hotel worker says.*

*Starlene Bray, a friend of the alleged victim, says the young woman is upset over a media stakeout outside her home in Eagle, Colo.*

*"She's kind of in hiding right now," Bray, 19, said on ABCNEWS' Good Morning America. "She's been back and forth from Denver, kind of trying to avoid the media and the press right now."*

*Bryant's accuser, a former high school cheerleader, says the 24-year-old NBA star sexually assaulted her on June 30 while he was staying at the hotel where she works. Prosecutors are now weighing whether to charge Bryant, who has denied the allegations.*

*The media has not released her name, but Bray says it seems as if everyone in the town of Eagle, a community of just 3,700 people, knows that her friend is the woman who has accused Bryant of sexual assault. And reports alleging the young woman has had emotional problems have made the attention even worse, Bray says.*

*A recent story in the Vail Daily newspaper reported that the young woman sought a doctor's care this spring for emotional problems that resulted from the death of a friend and a breakup. Bray says it's true that her friend did seek help, but she says that had nothing to do with the woman's allegations against Bryant.*

*"She did seek some medical help," Bray says. "She knew she needed it, so she went and got it. She was definitely emotionally fragile, but I don't think it had anything to do with what happened."*

*Meanwhile, a steady stream of reporters from around the country were circling the middle-class cul-de-sac where the young woman's home was located.*

*The woman had been described by her friends as a talented piano player. She sang in her high school choir and tried out for the FOX show "American Idol."*

*Officials at the Lodge & Spa at Cordillera in Edwards, Colo., where the young woman alleged the attack took place, say Bryant was a guest there June 30-July 2. Bryant, who is married and has a baby daughter, was in Colorado for knee surgery at a Vail clinic.*

*Bryant surrendered to authorities on July 4 and was released after posting $25,000 bond.*

## Bryant Proclaims Innocence

*Bryant denied the allegations and said he "would never do something like that," in a story printed in Sunday's Los Angeles Times. "When everything comes clean, it will all be fine, you'll see," Bryant said.*

*Bray says she has no doubts about her friend's story.*

*"Well, when I first talked to her, she seemed really distraught in the fact that it had happened to her," Bray said. "She didn't know what was going to happen to her. She was just scared."*

*Bray says her friend encouraged her to speak publicly "to tell everybody who she was and what kind of person she was and to try to get the newspapers and everything like that to settle down on her."*[1]

When Starlene's interview was over, she received a phone call from Kelly Hagen, a producer with *Inside Edition.* Hagen complimented Bray on her *Good Morning America* performance and asked if she would speak out for Lilly on her show. Starlene accommodated the New York producer, and two weeks later Hagen flew to Eagle to become better acquainted with Lilly's inner circle.

---

1. Copyright © ABC News, reprinted with permission.

Upon their return to Eagle, the couple was inundated by phone calls from the media asking for interviews. Luke Bray, who was becoming more interested in speaking out, chose to speak to FOX on account of his right-of-center political slant.

Rob Wheeler, one of the two attorneys hired by Lilly's parents, asked Luke not to specify what the rape evidence was, so he simply referred to it as "visible evidence." What most viewers, and Luke himself, didn't know was that he was about to become Lilly's most unlikely champion. Of all the people heartbroken about Bryant's arrest in Eagle, Luke Bray was among the most passionate. During the past few years of his young life, Luke had idolized Kobe Bryant as both a sports hero and role model for his generation. In many ways he related to Bryant, who, like himself, had married young and had a small child.

In keeping with his perception of Bryant, Luke lacked the temptation to cheat on his wife or fall out of line with the law. But now, seeing someone as stellar and as clean as Bryant fall from grace, confused him. The arrest prompted him to ponder his own potential to be corrupted and lose everything that was sacred to him. The very thought of it made him uneasy. It was too easy to make a mistake, he felt, to hurt someone you loved and lose everything you'd spent your whole life building.

In his own mind, Luke was somewhat disappointed with himself already. The moment a friend in Colorado Springs told him she'd heard that Bryant had been arrested, Bray told her that he wanted to drive downtown to bail Bryant out himself. Daunted, however, by the $25,000 amount, Bray had to settle for paying a visit instead to his son Nicholas in his room, where he tucked the boy in and then revisited his emotions of the past month.

At first he hadn't any idea who the alleged victim was. He didn't know her name, so he often thought of her as the

"stupid bitch," who had apparently "lost her fucking mind."
Initially, he hadn't even contemplated the possible criminal
penalties for Bryant because he was completely convinced
that his role model was innocent. Instead, Luke wondered
about the possible charges for defamation of character and
false accusation that Bryant could file against the woman
who'd told police the NBA player had raped her. Luke hoped
that Bryant would clear his name and then strike back for the
unwarranted attack he'd suffered.

Inside of Luke Bray's closet was a pair of Kobe Bryant
Adidas shoes and an L.A. Lakers jersey with the name
"Bryant" on the back. He recalled a moment when he was
standing on a snowy sidewalk in Denver waiting to see the
Lakers play the Denver Nuggets. He had spent hours in the
snow waiting to buy a ticket from someone, anyone, and
finally managed to gain entry into the arena just in time to see
Kobe Bean Bryant throw a basketball from half court
through the hoop. It was as if he'd been destined to arrive at
the launch of that one, perfect shot.

Bray's confusion arose shortly after Independence
Day when he was speaking to a friend who worked at
Cordillera. The friend mentioned that the girl who had
accused Kobe Bryant of sexual assault worked there as a
concierge and her last name was Fuller. Lifting an eyebrow,
Luke turned to his wife and asked her if Lilly had worked as
a concierge at Cordillera that summer.

When the Brays called their friend to ask if she was the
woman whom all America had been talking about, Lilly confirmed she was. Almost instantly, Bray shot back across the
phone, "Are you out of your fucking mind! You have no idea
what you're up against."

Bray hadn't yet stopped to consider the possibility
that Lilly had told police investigators the truth. He was more
concerned that "this would be the most significant black
mark on sports since the O.J. Simpson murder trial."

In the Simpson case, though, Luke felt the circumstances were different because the former NFL running back had long been retired. O.J.'s arrest and trial, which had dominated the nation's interest, was set against the background of possible police corruption in the wake of the anarchic Los Angeles riots.

In Bryant's case, he was a living, breathing, performing legend whose greatness the world was just beginning to witness. Now, his career could come to a devastating end, and as a Kobe fan, Bray felt let down. He admitted, "I'm not sure what to be angrier about; the fact that someone hurt my friend, or that it's the guy I admire most who did it."

While Luke was sitting at home with his son contemplating how the NBA would be affected by Bryant's possible conviction, he heard the front door open and saw a familiar face enter the room.

"Lilly," he said as he let out a deep, nervous breath. Lilly nodded and sat down on a sofa and glanced around the apartment. Afraid to continue looking at her, and worried that he would confirm his own suspicions and fears, Luke stared at the floor. Finally, he looked up and his eyes went to the abrasion on her neck where Lilly had told his wife that Bryant had choked her. (In court it was reported that the mark was half the size of a penny when in actuality the marks were more significant, having taken a few days to become fully bruised and visible.)

Inside, Luke Bray felt his hero-worship crumble. He had wanted to hate Lilly at that moment, wanted to blame her for destroying what he'd loved most in life, not just a player he admired, but a sense of dependency and trust, something he'd come to revere and respect. He was angry at Bryant. He was angry at himself. He hadn't really believed Lilly at first. He had hoped she was delusional. He had hoped she was lying. He had hoped for anything. He just wanted to see Bryant win another championship, and then another, and another.

Distraught, Luke wondered if there was anything or anyone he could count on in the world. When he looked around the room he noticed a photograph of his wife and daughter. He exhaled deeply, stood up and took a seat next to Lilly.

He turned his full attention on her.

"Why did you say no?" he asked. It was *Kobe Bryant*, Bray thought.

He looked at her closely now. This was it. This was the moment. *Why did she say no?*

Lilly opened her hands as if she lacked the words to explain, simply looked at Luke and said, "I just didn't want to."

Bray nodded silently.

"I only went in his room because I thought I'd get an autograph."

*That was it?* An autograph. *A fucking autograph?* Bray thought. Then he realized that's exactly what he would have done.

For Luke Bray, Kobe Bryant was no more.

# 7

## CRUEL INTENTIONS

Lilly Fuller felt a sense of safety in the Bray household. When Starlene invited her to stay with them for a few days, Lilly happily accepted. She'd been lonely in her bedroom at home and felt a need to escape the protective demands of her parents. For days on end, Lilly remained inside the Bray's apartment, playing board games with Starlene and with Nicholas, watching television and renting movies, while several journalists frantically searched town in an effort to find her. Luke, who had grown accustomed to the almost cozy situation as they sheltered themselves from the legions of reporters, described the experience as "riding out a storm."

The only journalist who was allowed access to the inner circle was Kelly Hagen from *Inside Edition* who, while visiting town, went river-rafting with the Brays. When she left, she asked the couple if they would be willing to again appear on her show, but they declined. They'd had enough of television interviews and wanted to try and get their lives back in order.

While Luke Bray was making amends with Lilly Fuller and coming to terms with his new perception of Kobe Bryant, several of Lilly's other "friends" were in the process of betraying her. Many of Lilly's former schoolmates passed along less than flattering stories to the press about her character, while others simply discovered that their romance with out-of-town journalists would be short-lived on account of the negative portrayal of Eagle and its most famous resident.

In one disastrous turn of events, a Fuller friend was lured into confessing that Lilly had attempted suicide two months earlier, in May, while staying with her family.

Lindsey McKinney, a former classmate who had become a confidante of Lilly's during the incident, inadvertently confirmed the suicide attempt when the reporter, calling from the Orange County Register, told her that she'd already confirmed the story elsewhere and just wanted to make sure her facts were accurate.

McKinney, thinking the story was about to come out anyway, talked to the reporter. Not knowing that everything she said was on the record unless she specifically stated it was "off the record," McKinney was quoted in the article and was perceived by those in the Fuller camp as having betrayed her dear friend.

McKinney redeemed herself, for a short time at least, when she refused the inducements of a reporter from *The National Enquirer* who offered to pay her to talk about her friend's personal life and previous near-death encounters. During a visit from the *Enquirer* reporter, she was told "we can offer $12,500, but the interview has to be tonight or tomorrow. For that we need exclusivity. You can't talk to anyone else in the media."

McKinney said nothing.

"We'll want a picture, preferably a picture with the victim," the reporter added. "Does that amount of money make a dent to you at all?"

"No, not really," McKinney responded.

"It's more than I've ever seen them pay for any-thing," the reporter said. "Stories on Julia Roberts only pay five grand."

McKinney declined, but was later surprised to learn that one of her friends pointed Lilly's photo out in the year-book to a tabloid reporter from New York. She was even more upset when another "friend" sold a personal photograph of Lilly to a reporter from Channel 7 for $10 because he needed gas money and a pack of cigarettes.

Strangely enough, several days later McKinney decided to supply a quote free of charge.

"She craves attention like no other," she said of Lilly. "This is the bad kind of attention that she's going to get. I'm not saying [the alleged rape] didn't happen. But it just doesn't fit the puzzle."

One of Lilly's former boyfriends, Josh Putnam, wasn't above selling out his former girlfriend in the national spotlight. In a rare opportunity for the Eagle High graduate to cash in on his 15 minutes of fame, Putnam didn't hesitate to tell the media that Lilly was a "total starve for attention."

"It doesn't matter if [the attention] was good or bad," Putnam said. "It was always good to her."

Sara Dabner, a 17-year old who told the wire service she looked up to Lilly as a big sister, struck back at Putnam, saying, "Why would a woman put herself through all of this—having people call her names? She's not trying to drag him through the dirt—she just wants justice."

Several days later Lilly became lonely while hiding in her bedroom at home and decided she would venture out with two of her closest friends, Bridgette Lowry and Nicole McDonough. Lilly didn't want to go anywhere where she would encounter too many people, but McDonough asked her if it would be all right if they stopped by the house of Steve Evancho, a former classmate.

Evancho was having a few friends over, and among them was Casey Smith, a local man who McDonough had developed an interest in. As soon as Evancho saw Lilly walk through the front door, he quickly alerted some of his friends.

Evancho and his friends—Casey Smith and T.J. Stanford—were Bryant fans and decided it would be worthwhile if they could get Lilly to admit something on tape.

Evancho ran into his bedroom and armed himself with a video camcorder and then struggled to find a videotape. When he walked into the other room, his friends were trying to coax Lilly into admitting something personal.

"Did it hurt, Lilly?" one of them asked. "Did it hurt?"

"Was it big?" another young man asked. "It was BIG, wasn't it?"

Lilly, who was becoming visibly upset, started to cry. Throwing her arms in the air, she shouted back, "Yeah it was big, okay!?" and ran out to the car. She couldn't believe anyone would say something like that to her. She was so angry she wanted to scream. She had never been mean to any of those people before. Why were they being so cruel to her now? Her friends soon joined her and took her home to the isolation of her bedroom.

Evancho couldn't load the tape into his camcorder because it became stuck. Disappointed, he decided to report an alternative version of the event to NBC.

## KOBE'S ACCUSER BRAGGED: PARTYGOER: SHE WAS HAPPY

### DEREK ROSE, THE NEW YORK DAILY NEWS, JULY 24, 2003

*The young woman accusing Kobe Bryant of rape bragged about the alleged assault at a party last week and gave a graphic description of the NBA star's anatomy, partygoers said. Steve Evancho told NBC News that he was surprised when the 19-year old woman showed up at his house party on July 15—three days before prosecutors slapped Bryant with sex assault charges.*

*"She was bragging about the whole thing," Evancho said, adding that the woman seemed "happy. She was having fun."*

*She even answered a question about the 6-foot-7 L.A. Laker's manhood, five people at the party told NBC.*

*"She answered a question with a gesture and description," said NBC correspondent Michelle Hofland. "They couldn't believe it."*[1]

Luke Bray couldn't believe it either. In fact, he didn't believe it. To him, the NBC report was "bullshit" and what his friends did to Lilly was "even more bullshit."

Later, when Smith was confronted by a reporter with the possibility that the event was filmed, he initially denied it. When the reporter asked Smith why he was telling people there was such a tape, the young man became angry and shouted, "because there is a tape!" Smith threatened the reporter with physical violence and then hung up the phone. A week later, he erupted into another argument with someone in a Denver parking lot and was stabbed with a knife.

Evancho on the other hand had begun to feel badly about the incident. During a local sporting event, he apologized to Luke Bray and told him that he regretted what he'd done. Bray, who was still annoyed, simply looked at Evancho and responded, "You're apologizing to the wrong person."

Little by little, Luke was becoming more frustrated with his friends' acting like immature teenagers and with their willingness to turn against someone they were supposed to remain loyal to. Bray knew that the NBC correspondent who reported the story had no way of knowing it was false, but what provoked him was that she certainly didn't know it was true either. The story prompted  him to consider

---

1. Copyright © New York Daily News, L.P. reprinted with permission.

how reporters balanced their stories. He wanted to know how decisions were made about what to report, and what to write off as rumor.

One pattern that he found questionable was the practice of media outlets republishing a story just because another media organization had already reported it. Bray found the practice irresponsible and wondered why reporters didn't investigate a story personally before running it. Having had little interaction with the press prior to the Bryant case, Bray wasn't familiar with the constitutional privileges that allowed journalists to republish information that had already appeared elsewhere, or that had been revealed in court.

Bray also wasn't familiar with "shield statutes," which protected a journalist's right to attribute reports to anonymous sources without revealing their identity. In time, however, he would learn about these strange practices, which seemed almost like tribal customs, part of a foreign culture that he'd have to study in order to survive.

One of the journalistic practices that Bray had become familiar with was the covenant that kept rape victims' identities out of the press. Bray was confused, however, when two media outlets violated that covenant by exposing Lilly's identity.

In California, a radio talk show host named Tom Leykis had revealed Lilly's full name after he read a newspaper article that detailed the names of her closest friends. Leykis defended his action by saying that he didn't think "you can have a fair trial where you know the name of one person and not the other."

Patricia Saunders, director of the Graham Windham Manhattan Mental Health Center in New York, criticized Leykis, saying, "This is a violation of privacy, and in that way, it is very much, psychologically, like a rape."

Shortly after Leykis finished preaching fairness, Lilly Fuller received a phone call from a college student at the University of Iowa.

# ACCUSER ALLEGEDLY GETS DEATH THREAT STUDENT CHARGED WITH PHONE THREAT ON ALLEGED KOBE VICTIM

## ASSOCIATED PRESS, AUGUST 22

IOWA CITY, Iowa, Aug. 22—*A University of Iowa student was charged with threatening to kill the woman accusing Kobe Bryant of sexual assault.*

*JOHN WILLIAM RICHE, 22, was arrested Thursday afternoon for allegedly leaving a profanity-laced message on the accuser's answering machine July 27, according to a federal grand jury indictment.*

*RICHE is charged with making a threatening telephone call across state lines. If convicted, he faces up to five years in prison and a $250,000 fine.*

*The caller threatened to assault the Eagle, Colo., woman with a coat hanger and repeatedly said he would kill her, the indictment said. Authorities did not say how the call was traced to RICHE.*

*A friend, Elliot Schwinn, described RICHE as a "sports fanatic" who had been drinking all day at a golf tournament when he allegedly made the call.*

*Jeff Dorschner, spokesman for the U.S. Attorney's Office in Denver, confirmed Bryant's accuser was the target but declined to comment further.*

*Roche appeared in federal court in Rock Island, Ill., late Thursday where he posted bond and was released, Dorschner said. He was ordered to appear Sept. 2 in U.S. District Court in Denver.*

*Bryant, 24, is charged with sexually assaulting a 19-year-old resort employee near Vail, Colo., on June 30. The Los Angeles Lakers star has said the sex was consensual.*

*Bryant's case has drawn widespread attention, including fan Web sites devoted to the case, some disclosing the identity of*

*Bryant's accuser. The judge handling the case has said some letters sent to authorities about the case have included death threats.*

*In Eagle, the accuser's father has called police twice in the past three weeks to report suspicious incidents, according to police records reviewed Friday.*

*In one, a police report said family members left two dogs at home the morning of Aug. 14. When they returned about an hour later, the more aggressive dog was locked in an upstairs bathroom, apparently by an intruder. Nothing was missing and there were no signs of forced entry, according to the police report.*

*On July 30, police records show, the woman's father said a man stopped at the house and offered to wash the windows. When the father refused, the man left without stopping at any nearby homes, police were told.*"[1]

Several days later a Swiss man with supposed ties to the Russian mafia was arrested in Los Angeles for contacting Bryant's security detail and offering to "take care of Kobe's problem" for $3 million. Patrick Graber, a 31-year-old body-builder, offered Bryant and his camp his services in killing Lilly for a mere $1 million down and $2 million after the job was complete. Defense attorney Peter Knecht described Graber as "a little bit naive and not very swift. He is not the most intelligent guy in the world."

Shortly after the death threats, Luke wondered if Leykis still thought that his having revealed Lilly's identity had helped balance the scales of "fairness." But Leykis wasn't the only one exposing Lilly. Almost simultaneously, the *Globe* tabloid made a decision to put her photograph on its cover for an issue on sale at nearly every supermarket checkout in America. The photo, which featured Lilly in a dark blue denim jacket, smiling broadly with neatly layered blonde hair to her shoulders, was taken directly out of her senior high school yearbook. A conspicuous black bar masked her eyes.

---

1. Reprinted with the permission of the Associated Press.

When the tabloid hit the checkout lines, its editorial director, Jim Lynch, told the *New York Daily News*, "This is the number one face in America that people want to see, and so we decided to go with it." The photograph, which dominated nearly the entire cover of the tabloid, astounded those who knew Lilly but didn't realize she was Bryant's alleged victim.

Johnray Strickland, a sophomore at University of Northern Colorado in Greeley who had dated Lilly shortly before summer vacation, noticed the tabloid in a supermarket checkout line in Las Vegas, where he was visiting his parents for the summer. Almost instantly, he pulled out his cell phone and called Lilly to ask her if she was the alleged victim in the Bryant case.

"Is that really you?" Strickland asked.

Lilly, who hadn't seen the cover, asked him what he was talking about.

"I think this is your face on the cover of the *Globe*," he told her. "It says that you're the girl who got attacked by Kobe Bryant."

Lilly, who didn't know about the tabloid cover yet, became agitated. She confirmed for her former boyfriend that she was indeed the woman he was talking about, and then told him she wanted to run to the supermarket to see the cover.

"You never called me after summer vacation started," she added. "You should have stayed in touch with me."

Strickland, who now felt badly, searched for something to say. "I'm sure I'll see you at school in the fall," he said.

Lilly, who wasn't sure she was returning, told Strickland she'd probably see him in the fall.

When Strickland hung up the phone, he wondered if he would have ever known she was the victim had the *Globe* not published the photograph. He also wondered how many other people would now recognize her.

The *Globe's* decision not to protect an alleged rape victim's identity prompted a hue and cry from some journalists and critics. For several days afterward, the issue was debated on television talk shows. Some critics said they agreed with Tom Leykis, that in order to have a fair trial, a person's Sixth Amendment right to face his or her accuser applied to the court of public opinion and not just that of a court of law.

Three months later, the *Globe* ran Lilly's full photograph on their cover without the black bar that had shielded her eyes the first time, along with her full name. In an astonishing move, Karen DeCrow, the former president of the National Organization of Women, defended the action.

"By not naming a rape victim, the media and legal system perpetuate the belief that the alleged victim has done something wrong, that the rape was somehow her fault."

Lilly, who later heard about the quote, wrote the DeCrow viewpoint off as absurd. She hadn't felt she had done anything wrong—all she wanted was her privacy and for the death threats to stop.

DeCrow wasn't alone, however.

Also quoted by the *Globe* was Susan Brownmiller, a feminist who told the publication that naming rape victims in court should be "standard procedure."

Krista Flannigan, an attorney and victim's consultant working for the Eagle County District Attorney's Office felt otherwise. Flannigan told the press in an interview that among the feelings rape victims have are, "Fear, anxiety, some form of guilt, sadness, anger, vulnerability—those come and go," she said. "Some are more intense than others, depending on what their past life experiences have been, what their current support systems are, what their past support systems have been." A high-profile, public case, Flannigan argued, can affect the victim and her family with greater intensity.

In an attempt to escape the tabloids and their so-called "sources," Lilly accepted an invite from a college friend to visit her family in Canada. While the two were in Calgary, they went out to restaurants and bars with some of her friends.

Lilly thought she'd finally escaped the tabloids when a strange man confronted her one night as she walked across the dance floor at a local nightclub.

"Don't you think you should be home studying when you're already on academic probation?" he said.

Lilly was speechless. A thousand scenarios rushed through her mind. She ran to her friends, and they immediately fled the club. At first, she assumed the man was from a tabloid, but then a more frightening possibility occurred to her: he might be an investigator for Kobe Bryant.

When the Bryant investigators got wind of the incident they dispatched their own team to track down the mysterious man. After a short investigation they determined that he was simply a local man who was friends with the girl Lilly was staying with. It was clear that the media scrutiny was getting the best of the 19-year-old.

Another night, while with friends in a restaurant, a woman approached one of her group and tried to take some photos. Lilly was sure it was *The National Enquirer*. In a late-October edition of the tabloid, the *Enquirer* reported that Bryant's investigators had trailed Lilly to Calgary and interviewed people about her supposed wild behavior at a bar. What Lilly didn't know was that the girl she was staying with had a close friend who was detailing Lilly's every move to the *Enquirer*.

One of Lilly's college friends who heard from the press was her school roommate, Mandy Ross, who received a phone call from the *New York Post*. Ross, who was extremely protective of Lilly, declined the *Post*'s invitation to share information about her friend, and she asked the reporter to respect Lilly's privacy.

When she returned home to Eagle, Lilly once again sought sanctuary from the prying supermarket tabloids. She also was anxious to see Brian and Katie Fowler, two of her old high school friends. The couple, who lived in Gypsum, had a small child and like most locals often spent time with their former classmates. Lilly felt comfortable around her inner circle of friends and was happy to see the Fowlers. Unfortunately, what she didn't know was that Brian had recently revealed to a close friend that he was "talking to a guy from *The National Enquirer*."

The same *Enquirer* reporter tried calling Luke Bray to confirm some personal items about Lilly, but Luke became suspicious and asked him where he worked. He told Luke he wrote for "American Media," a publication that didn't ring a bell with him. Unaware that American Media was the conglomerate that owned all seven supermarket tabloids (*The National Enquirer, Star, Globe, The Examiner, The Sun, Weekly World News,* and *Mira!*), Luke stayed on the phone for a few minutes to listen to what he had to say, but, sensing something was wrong, finally declined an interview.

Soon after Lilly returned from Canada, the *Enquirer* published a new Kobe Bryant story about Lilly which was their harshest and most virulent to date. Three college students, whom Lilly later said she hardly knew, reported to the *Enquirer* that she was promiscuous and irresponsible, and liked to drink and use narcotics.

The three men, Ryan Wong, Steve Ward and Robert Macanic, all told lurid tales of Lilly offering sexual favors to them, drinking vodka straight from the bottle in a school hallway and using illegal drugs on a regular basis. The three men had their photographs taken and were quoted throughout the cover story, which portrayed Lilly as a young woman who enjoyed sleeping with multiple partners and had "a lot of emotional problems."

When Lilly first read the *Enquirer* interviews, she threw the tabloid down and burst into tears. She was hurt by the accusations, but what upset her even more was that she hardly even remembered who the three students were. When she returned to school in the fall, she ran into Steve Ward, only vaguely recognizing him. Ward apologized to her and told her that the tabloid reporter had simply misquoted him. Lilly looked at Ward for a moment in disbelief, and then turned and walked away.

# 8

## FULL COURT PRESS

When Kobe Bryant finally arrived for his August advisement (to advise Bryant of his rights and charges) with an entourage of sports utility vehicles in tow, he stepped out of his SUV and extended his hand to help his lead female attorney, Pamela Mackey, onto the curb. His bodyguards, Jose Revilla and Michael Ortiz, flanked him. Sporting a casual off-white Armani blazer and slacks, Bryant left the top button of his white oxford shirt unbuttoned and was without a tie. While most reporters stood quietly watching the 6-foot-7 NBA player walk inside, some members of the public shouted support.

"Stand tall, Kobe!" shouted one man.

"We believe in you, Kobe!" yelled another.

Among the many supporters for Bryant were two acquaintances of Lilly Fuller who showed up wearing Lakers jerseys. Jessica Willenberg and Janelle Medina had also painted their faces with purple and yellow paint, while their cars were plastered with slogans like, "Kobe is innocent!"

When one journalist asked the girls why they believed Bryant over their former classmate, one of them responded, "Kobe Bryant is so hot he wouldn't need to rape anyone."

Several television crews interviewed the Eagle High grads, and broadcast their opinions.

While Willenberg and Medina were aligning themselves with the athlete, two of Lilly's other friends found jobs with national television networks. Nicole Yandle, whose sister Rachel began dating Lilly's former boyfriend Matthew Herr, accepted a position with NBC. Amy Rammunno, whose step-mother, Cindy Rammunno worked for the *Vail Daily*, and whose step-grandmother was Eagle's mayor, Roxy Deane, took cues from ABC.

Once the advisement started, most reporters who weren't inside the small courtroom flocked to the press tent where they watched the proceedings on banks of TVs brought in by county employees.

Inside the courtroom Bryant sat calmly beside his attorneys. After all of the anticipation, he would utter only two words throughout the entire proceedings—"No, sir."

## BRYANT GOES TO COURT
## HEARING SET FOR OCTOBER;
## JUDGE SEEKS PROBE OF LEAKS

### HOWARD PANKRATZ, LEGAL AFFAIRS WRITER, THE DENVER POST, AUGUST 6, 2003

EAGLE—*County Judge Frederick Gannett formally advised basketball superstar Kobe Bryant on Wednesday that he is accused of sexual assault and announced that a special investigator is being appointed to look into alleged leaks of information in the case. The 24-year-old Bryant, dressed in a light-colored suit and displaying no sign of nervousness, sat and then stood quietly, his hands folded in front of him with his two lawyers beside him. He appeared to take no notice of the crowds gathered outside the courthouse, though many of the people who turned out were his fans.*

*During the late Wednesday afternoon hearing, most of the 69 courtroom seats were filled with the media, general public and members of the district attorney's staff. About 16 other people, staff at the Eagle County courthouse, filled the jury box.*

*Gannett didn't read the text of the charge; one of Bryant's attorneys, Pamela Mackey, said Bryant would waive the reading.*

*The charge accuses Bryant of using physical force or violence to coerce a young woman to have sex with him the night of June 30. The sexual assault allegedly occurred at the Lodge & Spa at Cordillera—about 17 miles from Eagle, where the woman lives.*

*Bryant has admitted that he committed adultery that night but has claimed that the alleged victim had consensual sex with him.*

*At the advisement, Mackey requested a preliminary hearing for Bryant and said Bryant would waive the 30-day rule, which usually requires the hearing to be held within that time.*

*Gannett asked Bryant if he had any problems with waiving the 30-day requirement. Bryant, in a calm voice, said, "No, sir."*

*The judge announced that Bryant's preliminary hearing will be held at 1 p.m. Oct. 9."*[1]

As Bryant left the courthouse, most reporters retreated to their respective media tents and began filing their reports. Two, however, ran to their car instead and began to trail Bryant to the Eagle County Airport. Bryant, riding in the middle of three sports utility vehicles, avoided Interstate-70 and instead took Highway 6, which broke through the rocky mountain canyons beside Eagle River, a small stream running east and west.

---

1. Copyright © *The Denver Post*, reprinted with permission.

When Bryant arrived at the airport, his troupe cruised through an iron gate right onto the runway. The two reporters following attempted the same but were halted by an airport security officer who told them they weren't permitted access to the runway without authorization from the tower. As Bryant descended from a red and white SUV, the two reporters unsuccessfully tried to gain access by running through an abandoned part of the airport which ended up being locked. Then, within a matter of seconds, the jet's cabin door closed and the plane cruised up the runway and ascended from the tiny town of Eagle.

As the journalists watched, one quipped, "If Kobe Bryant doesn't ever see Eagle, Colorado again, I don't think he'll be the least bit disappointed."

# 9

## JUST THE BEGINNING

Roslyn Anderson, a New York City transplant and one of Eagle's only African-American residents, sat quietly in the back of the Brush Creek Saloon. Anderson, who had moved to Colorado after a brief stint as a show-tunes dancer in Manhattan, was friendly with the Brays and had recently met Lilly Fuller. She'd seen the abrasions on Lilly's neck.

"He went too far," she said to a friend. "He went too far."

A man known only to those in the bar as "Wild Bill," held court for a variety of journalists who were looking for a colorful local perspective. The bartender, Janet, who was used to mainly dealing with locals, was now serving a host of professional reporters from across the United States. A few Eagle locals shot a game of pool in the back of the tiny saloon, uninterested in talking about their town's most recent claim to fame.

While the press was prowling the streets and businesses of Eagle, Lilly and her parents had a strange encounter from on-high when a helicopter began hovering only 30 feet above their house. As the family struggled to hear themselves think over the throbbing racket, a neighbor who was a private pilot called the Eagle Airport Control Tower to have him patched through to the pilot. The neighbor began screaming at the pilot that he was in clear violation of FAA regulations and laws, but was astounded when the pilot justified his actions by saying they were taking photographs of the Fuller home.

It was unknown to whom the California-registered helicopter belonged, but the family's lawyers also noticed the same helicopter hovering near their homes as well. Shortly after the incident, the Fuller family left for a couple of hours, leaving their two golden retrievers wandering the house as usual. When they returned, they found the dogs locked in an upstairs bathroom. Lilly, who knew that the dogs would never wander into that bathroom of their own accord (it was where their forced baths took place), was convinced someone had been inside her home. When she ran to her room she noticed that her diaries had been moved and were left open. It was as if someone wanted her to know they had been there.

* * *

Johnray Strickland was sitting in his college dorm room when he received a phone call from a reporter for CBS' *48 Hours* in New York City. The reporter had fielded an e-mail that Strickland had sent the network. He was able to verify that Strickland was in fact Lilly Fuller's former boyfriend from college, and began interviewing him via telephone.

During the conversation, Strickland relayed that Lilly was an honest person who would never send an innocent person to prison. The reporter offered to fly him to Manhattan for an interview with one of CBS's top journalists, Lesley Stahl.

While Strickland was contemplating speaking out for his former girlfriend, Lilly Fuller was discussing her future plans with her lawyers and parents in her Eagle home only a few miles away. The college sophomore was determined to return to school, and her parents wanted her to do the same. Although Fuller wanted to resume her studies, her main reason was to avoid the social isolation of her bedroom at home. But first she had agreed to meet with Strickland to talk about his defense of her. Driving in her small sedan, she headed out to Interstate-70, to Greeley, where Johnray Strickland waited for her.

Once she arrived, the two discussed the possibility of Strickland speaking out on her behalf. She could tell that he wanted to defend her and together they contemplated the best-case scenario. Since Strickland knew the *48 Hours* reporter, they decided that CBS seemed the least likely to attack her. After recalling a conversation with her lawyers, Lilly told Strickland that he could not talk about the evidence, particularly what happened inside the room, but that he could discuss how Bryant led her up to his room and blocked the door on the way out.

## FULL COURT PRESS

### *48 HOURS INVESTIGATES*, OCTOBER 4, 2003

*"There is no doubt in my mind that she has been taken advantage of by Kobe Bryant. There is no doubt in my mind that Kobe Bryant raped my friend," says Johnray Strickland, who is talking to 48 Hours Investigates because his friend, Bryant's accuser, can't.*

*Correspondent Lesley Stahl reports.*

*Strickland is a 19-year-old college sophomore at the University of Northern Colorado. His friendship with Bryant's accuser began last spring after they met at a party. Strickland says they dated for a while, and they remain close friends.*

*"She wanted somebody to come out and really stand up for her. And people have been really, really treating her like the bad guy in this, when she definitely is not,"* says Strickland. *"She is really a victim in this. It's just she's been represented as an accuser, which is true. She is an accuser. But she, she is a victim as well."*

That's exactly right, according to Eagle County District Attorney Mark Hurlbert, who has charged Bryant, 25, with felony sexual assault. If he's convicted, the NBA superstar could face life in prison.

*"I feel that after reviewing the evidence, after looking at the evidence, I can prove this case beyond a reasonable doubt,"* says Hurlbert.

48 Hours Investigates went undercover where the alleged rape took place, at the Lodge and Spa at Cordillera. Kobe Bryant checked into the exclusive Colorado resort on June 30, and Strickland's 19-year-old friend was working the front desk as a receptionist that night.

She gave Bryant the standard tour of the spa. Then, Strickland says, Bryant invited her to his room, where she went willingly. At some point, sources say, he wound up with his hands around her neck, causing some injuries, pushed her down onto a bed or a couch in his room and then allegedly raped her.

*"I'm innocent. You know, I didn't force her to do anything against her will. I'm innocent,"* said Bryant at a July news conference that surprised many since the conference was given just hours after the Eagle District attorney filed charges against the NBA star.

At the news conference, Vanessa, Bryant's 21-year-old wife, was at her husband's side, where she has remained since the incident. But Bryant shocked everyone when he admitted one thing: *"I sit here in front of you guys furious at myself, disgusted at myself for making a mistake of adultery."*

Bryant and his lawyer, Pamela Mackey, are vowing to fight the charges all the way. Both are under the gag order and refused our request for an interview.

"*I do not believe the charges should have been filed in this case,*" says Mackey. "*The evidence does not support it.*" "*These cases, acquaintance rape cases more than any other kind of crime, rise and fall on the candor and credibility of that young lady who is making the charge,*" says Linda Fairstein, a former prosecutor of sexual crimes in New York City, and a consultant to 48 Hours Investigates.

Fairstein has spoken with sources in Colorado who have seen the alleged victim's medical report. The report, she says, includes some evidence of bruising on the neck.

What about the medical exam? Did she go to the hospital the next day?

"*Yes, she went to the hospital. She was examined by a nurse,*" says Fairstein. "*There are reports that there are minor lacerations, vaginally.*"

But Fairstein says the medical report and other information suggest the internal injuries were not very serious: "*There is no physician on the witness list. So I assume there was nothing serious enough.*"

In any case, Fairstein says that Bryant's defense team will undoubtedly have experts to dispute the meaning of any medical evidence. And they will only put their client on the stand if they need to.

"*You know, he has no obligation to do anything,*" says Fairstein. "*By human nature, people like to hear what they call both sides of the story.*"

But Fairstein says the jury will decide this case on the credibility of the accuser. And Bryant's attorneys will do everything they can to undermine it. They have already subpoenaed her unrelated medical records relating to possible suicide attempts.

"*The mental history is entirely different from the sexual history. And yes, if they can uncover something that is evidence, and I assume they're looking for instability—and instability related to credibility—then they will certainly be able to cross-examine her about it,*" says Fairstein.

*Strickland confirmed that his friend did try to commit suicide twice: "I think we have all moved on from that. And that was a dark time. And we had to go through that. And now we're through with it."*

*How does Strickland think his friend will do under the pressure?*

*"I think my friend is the strongest individual I've ever met. I think that she is actually getting stronger as the days go by,"* he says. *"That things are just, she can handle the trial. She can handle this."*

*"Basketball will survive, but you know, this won't be one of its more fun years,"* says Los Angeles Times sports columnist Mark Heisler, who has known Kobe Bryant for years.

*In fact, Heisler has known Kobe since his father, Joe "Jellybean" Bryant, was a professional basketball player himself. Then, Heisler covered the son, who went right from high school to a multi-million-dollar-a-year deal with the NBA, skipping college.*

*"I think ultimately it turned out it was the wrong decision. And I think that's what we're talking about now,"* says Heisler. *"You know, a young guy who even if he was ready for the basketball part of it, wasn't ready for the life part of it."*

*In seven seasons with the Los Angeles Lakers, Bryant and his teammates have won three championships.*

*"He's a tremendous player. He's a gifted player. He's an exciting player. He's a wild player,"* says Heisler.

*Bryant is a wild player who is paid roughly $12.5 million a year by the Los Angeles Lakers. He earns another $10 million to $12 million a year from endorsements. But none of his basketball success really matters now.*

*"I think he's basically just walled himself off. I think Kobe is more miserable now than he's ever been in his life,"* says Heisler. *"The real tragedy for Kobe is that this is a guy who really meant to do the right thing. And to be the guy. And to be the role model."*

*But if this case goes to court and Bryant is convicted of sexual assault, the 25-year-old NBA star may spend the rest of his life in prison.*

*Does Strickland's friend want to see Bryant in jail?* "My friend wants to see justice done. Whatever his, his sentence is. Anything. She just wants to see justice carried out," says Strickland.

*Would she mind seeing him behind bars?* "She wouldn't. I think she would love it because of how scared she is of him," says Strickland. "She is terrified of him."

*Did Bryant hurt her? Was she in pain?*

"She was subjected to physical harm," says Strickland. "She felt pain."

*How did he find out what happened?*

"A friend called me. And I was living in Las Vegas, actually, when this happened. So he called me and he asked me some questions about this girl that I started dating at the end of the school year," says Strickland. "And then he said, 'Well, you should go look at The Globe.' So I went to The Globe and there she was. And then I called her, and of course her reaction was, 'I was waiting for you to figure that out.'"

*Strickland learned much more of what happened that night from his former girlfriend, some of which he shared with 48 Hours Investigates. He says it began when his friend gave Bryant the standard tour of the Cordillera Lodge.*

"He asked her, 'Can you take me back to my room?' She agreed. It was, you know, take her back to Room 35. And she was invited in. She stayed in the room for approximately around five minutes. And she wanted to leave, because she had to go back to work," says Strickland. "She actually had to clock out and go home that night. But when she tried to inform him that she had to leave and tried to leave, he blocked her way. He stood in front of her so she couldn't leave."

*At his friend's request, Strickland wouldn't say more about what happened in Room 35 the night of June 30.*

*But there are happier things about his friend he wants people to know.*

"She's just a beautiful person on the inside and out. She brings people in like no one else can. And she just trusts and allows people into her life. But sometimes, that leads to bad things," says Strickland.

"She trusted him just like she trusted me. Just like she would trust anyone. And trusted him most of all because . . . it was told to her before this that he was married."

Strickland says his friend has no interest in being paid off by Bryant, disputing reports that the Bryant camp attempted to make a civil settlement in the case: "No one tried to settle. No one tried to settle for $5 million."

For any amount? "There was no settlement. No settlement. No offer," says Strickland. "All she wants is she wants to see justice done. That's really all she wants."

Strickland confirmed that his friend tried to commit suicide twice, and one attempt was less than two months before the alleged rape.

"She's a completely stable person," he says. "These things had happened to her. But she has been through so much. And she is continuing to go through so much." Just weeks ago, Bryant's people turned in Patrick Graber after he allegedly offered to kill Strickland's friend for $3 million.

And there were reports of harassment. "We were actually sitting and watching a movie when she got the phone call. And we stopped everything. And we heard, she got off the phone and she said, 'You know, somebody broke into my house,'" says Strickland. "And we figured out later that all of her diaries had been moved. Nothing was stolen."

Strickland thinks somebody was trying to dig up dirt on his friend: "They're trying to find something. Anything. They're clawing for information to discredit this girl." More than anything, Strickland's friend wants him to debunk some of the outrageous stories being spread by the tabloids tales of her being promiscuous, a big party girl, always coming on to guys.

*And these are stories that Strickland denies as well.*

*Bryant's accuser doesn't have to appear in person at next week's pretrial hearing. But she will be the star witness in her videotape statement that she gave to police.*

*"You know, I tell her that once this is done, once this is all over, once the trial finishes, let's put some closure on it," says Strickland. "When you walk out of that courtroom, I don't want you to feel any weight. I don't want you to feel any pressure. It's closure. It's finished."*

*If Bryant goes to trial and gets convicted, he could face anywhere from 10 years probation to life in prison. Sentencing would be up to the judge.*

*Under Colorado law, Bryant is looking at a Class 3 felony—sexual assault including the use of physical force or threats. But his accuser did not necessarily have to resist for Bryant to be found guilty.*

*In bringing these charges, Bryant's accuser has stepped into an arena where the spotlight is intense. If there is a trial, both the young woman and Bryant will be sharing that spotlight—and the enormous pressure—for many months to come."*[1]

When *Full Court Press* aired on CBS, Lilly Fuller watched with great interest and intensity. She sat beside Johnray Strickland in her dorm room, surrounded by a cadre of supportive friends who cheered. When the show was finished, Strickland was thrilled. He felt as if he had accomplished something. To his dismay, however, Lilly was speechless. She thanked him quietly for his support and stood motionless. Later, Lilly would tell him that she was "just shocked to see a whole hour of national television devoted to me." It scared her when she saw the reality of so many people talking about her for so long.

Strickland nodded at her and thought, *You'd better get used to it Lilly, this is just the beginning.*

---

1. Copyright © CBS, reprinted with permission.

# 10[1]

## NO

When Lilly arrived at work at 3 p.m. on June 30, she was expecting yet another quiet evening at the Cordillera. Trapped at the apex of the local mountains, surrounded by vacation homes, Lilly Fuller and her few co-workers were almost alone during the off-season of a hot June in Colorado. Lilly took her seat at the desk near the front entrance to the lobby. Another concierge's table was across from her. On her desk was a phone, a computer and several information packets about the resort.

Lilly received a phone call from a travel agent who told her that two men named Javier and David Rodriguez would be staying at the hotel and to ready a series of rooms. After talking with the agent, Lilly learned that Javier Rodriguez was actually Kobe Bean Bryant, a name that she recalled from somewhere.

After a few other employees talked about Bryant's professional career and his celebrity status, Lilly became excited.

---

1. See Authors' Note (i).

Knowing that some of her closest friends loved sports, she thought they would be thrilled to hear that she had met a famous sports celebrity. Lilly knew, however, that the Cordillera had a strict policy of speaking to celebrity guests only when spoken to, since they came to the resort to escape their public identity.

Among the employees on duty that night was Trina McKay, who worked as the night auditor. Lilly had never spoken to the woman. She tried smiling, but McKay seemed to pay no attention to her. Lilly didn't understand why everyone couldn't be polite, but she often noticed that some women, particularly the older ones, didn't seem to be as friendly toward her as others.

The night moved slowly, and Lilly looked at the clock in anticipation of meeting Kobe Bryant. If anything, she could tell her friends that she saw him, how tall he really was and, at least, if he seemed like a nice guy. She was sure that he was. Although she didn't know much about him, most of her co-workers, particularly Bobby Pietrack, seemed to think that Kobe Bryant was a great guy, a star athlete of the highest physical prowess who had strong ethics and a deep respect for his family.

Earlier, someone from the Cordillera housing division had dropped off a brown envelope of information for Bryant. The envelope was addressed to "Mr. & Mrs. Bryant," which obviously meant the basketball hero was married. At the very least, she would have the opportunity to hand him the envelope. She was sure to get a smile. While waiting, she dug out a Sharpie marker and a sturdy Cordillera envelope. If she could move fast, maybe she could get an autograph to show her friends.

Although Bryant was expected to arrive at the hotel sometime shortly after 9 p.m., he did not. Bryant and his entourage, including his security men, Michael Ortiz and Troy Laster, mistakenly drove to the wrong hotel—"The

Lodge," in Vail Village. Hotel employees at The Lodge tried talking Bryant into staying there, but Bryant and the others decided that the privacy of Cordillera was worth the trip into the small hamlet of Edwards. The decision to relocate to the remote lodge and spa would be one to haunt him for the rest of his days.

After entering the small, gated community at the crest of a bank of mountains, Bryant and his team pulled up to the front of the hotel where the bellman, Bobby Pietrack, helped unload their luggage. Meanwhile, Lilly Fuller did her job. Gracious and poised, she approached Bryant with a smile and welcomed him to the Cordillera.

At Cordillera, it was customary to escort high profile guests to their rooms before checking them in. Lilly, who knew this procedure well, flashed her best smile and offered to show Bryant to his room. It was her job.

As she escorted Bryant, she couldn't help feeling a little surrounded by the athlete's entourage. Bryant, who chatted with her, seemed very friendly.

"That's a nice tattoo," Bryant said. Lilly laughed.

"Thanks," she said, looking at the flower on her ankle.

Once they arrived at the room, Bryant's bodyguards entered while Bryant and Lilly stood at the threshold of the door. Lilly, who noticed Ortiz and Laster scanning the room for something, felt Bryant's hand grip her right forearm.

Then, in a whisper, Bryant leaned down while flashing a brilliant grin and said, "Listen, do you think you can show me around a little later? Can you come back, if you don't mind?"

As Lilly looked into his eyes, she noticed a small flicker. She felt as if he really wanted her to show him around, and her pulse raced. She was flattered. He really liked her. She would get that autograph after all.

After a polite laugh, Lilly smiled and assured the NBA player that she would return after informing the front desk that she was giving a guest a tour. Bryant nodded and smiled.

Lilly and Bryant's bodyguards walked to the front desk to collect their keys and then to rooms 18 and 20 where they would be staying. Their job would be to act as guards for the remainder of the evening, blocking access to anyone walking toward Bryant's room.

"So, is Kobe Bryant pretty popular around here?" Ortiz asked while smiling at his partner, Laster. Laster smiled back. That was old hat to them. Lilly shrugged.

"Yeah, sure, I guess so," she said.

"You know who he is, don't you?" Laster asked incredulously.

"Yeah, sure," Lilly said. "He plays for the Los Angeles Lakers."

Laster nodded. "He's the best player in the NBA, did you know that?" Ortiz added.

Lilly nodded slightly. Feeling strange, she walked back to the front desk where she finished some quick paperwork. A few minutes later, she told Pietrack she was going back to Bryant's room to show him around the hotel. Pietrack, who seemed annoyed, told Lilly to use the quicker, outdoor path and to avoid the hallways where Bryant's bodyguards were. Lilly didn't know it, but Pietrack had just tried to go down one of the guarded hallways to get to another part of the hotel, and one of the men stood in his way, demanding he take another route. Pietrack wasn't very pleased with their lack of politeness.

Lilly scooted back to her desk, slipped her Sharpie marker and paper in her pocket and walked outside into the starry Colorado night. When she came to the heavy, wooden door on the outside of the lodge, she grasped the black, iron handle, opened the door, and walked down the hallway. When she arrived at Room 35, she took a deep breath and knocked on the door. After a moment, Bryant, dressed in blue Nike track pants, sneakers and a plain white T-shirt, answered.

"Well, are you ready?" Lilly asked, in anticipation of the tour. Bryant smiled and nodded.

Lilly couldn't wait to tell her friends. Here she was, showing Kobe Bryant around. As she pointed out the workout room and the spa to Bryant in the downstairs levels, he looked at her, seeming interested in something. Lilly laughed, nervously. They walked outside to the pool area, and Bryant walked over and looked at the Jacuzzi, which was covered with a tarp and closed for the evening. Bryant knelt down slowly, uttering a painful groan and said, "Boy, I'd love to get in here. It would sure help out my knee."

Lilly shrugged and explained that she didn't have the authority to open the hot tub. Bryant nodded as the two walked up an outdoor staircase to a deck.

"That's a nice dress you're wearing," Bryant said.

Lilly smiled and said, "Thank you."

As the two talked on the balcony, Bobby Pietrack walked outside to greet them. Lilly, who was happy to see Bobby, introduced him to Bryant. Pietrack, who played college basketball, smiled and shook Bryant's hand. The two men discussed sports for a few minutes and Lilly listened and wondered if this might be an appropriate moment to ask Bryant for his autograph.

When Pietrack noticed some new guests entering the lobby, he hurriedly said goodbye and ran inside to tend to his customers.

"Hey, you know something?" Bryant asked while looking around, "I'm not sure I know how to get back to my room from here. Think you can help me out?"

The two laughed, and Lilly nodded.

"Sure," she said.

As they walked back to his room, Bryant changed the tone of the conversation.

"So, do you have a boyfriend?" he asked.

The question took Lilly aback. She smiled and told the NBA player that she did not. At that moment, she thought of Bobby Pietrack. She knew that Bobby had a girlfriend, but she liked him. He seemed so friendly and sweet. She had known him for so long and she knew she could trust him. For some reason, she wished Bobby was right there with her then. She suddenly felt a little strange, but she couldn't put her finger on why.

"You know, a beautiful girl like you should really have a boyfriend," Bryant said.

Lilly's eyes widened. Did he just say what she thought he said? She had never thought she was beautiful. She didn't even think she was pretty. She had always been suspicious of the boys who had liked her. Now, for some reason, a famous celebrity who was married, was suddenly complimenting her? It made her feel wonderful.

"You're a nice height and a nice shape," Bryant said, interrupting her self-evaluation.

Lilly quietly thanked him.

When they reached his room, Bryant slipped his key into the door and unlocked it. Jarring the door open, he extended his arm as if he expected the conversation to continue, and casually asked, "Would you like to come in for a minute?"

Lilly paused. Was this a smart move? She still hadn't received that autograph.

She recalled the envelope that read, "Mr. and Mrs. Bryant" but noticed he was not wearing a wedding band.

(Since Lilly Fuller was not familiar with Kobe Bryant's career, she was unaware of how frequently he was known for wearing his wedding ring. Bryant was typically famous among other players for flaunting the ring when propositioned by women after games to indicate that he was married and uninterested in extra-marital activities.)

Assuring herself everything was okay, she went inside.

"Take a seat," Bryant said, pointing to a sofa across the room. Lilly walked across the suite.

"Do you have any other tattoos?" Bryant asked. Lilly nodded and told Bryant the story about the time she got a small rose tattooed on her back. As she removed her blazer to sit down, she turned around and adjusted her top about an inch so Bryant could see a rose on her back.

"Nice," Bryant said as he sat down in a chair.

As the two talked about Bryant's life in Los Angeles, he changed the subject to Cordillera and raised the issue of the Jacuzzi again.

"We should go down there and take a little dip," Bryant suggested. Lilly laughed and threw her arms up.

"I told you," she said, "I can't open it. Besides I don't have a bathing suit."

"That's okay with me," Bryant said, raising his left eyebrow and smiling.

Suddenly, Lilly Fuller felt the need to leave. Something was wrong. Something was very wrong. In her mind, this had gone beyond simple flirting.

"Listen, I really need to clock out," Lilly said, looking at her watch. Pulling out her marker and envelope, she asked the NBA star for an autograph.

Bryant, who looked down at the pen, pursed his lips as if he were pondering and then smiled.

"Why don't you come back up after you clock out and I'll sign it for you then," he said.

Lilly's smile dropped. What was he doing? It would take all but five seconds to sign his name. Lilly nodded and stood up. As she did, Bryant rose as well. At that moment, Lilly was conscious of how incredibly tall he was. It wasn't that she hadn't noticed it before, but for some reason, he seemed larger now.

"Can I have a hug?" he asked. Lilly nodded and slowly let Bryant embrace her. As he held her in his arms, Bryant tilted his head slightly and brushed her lips with his. As he kissed her, Lilly felt a wave of powerlessness come over her. He moved down her mouth and to her neck and she wondered what to do. In the back of her mind, she still couldn't believe someone so famous would be this interested in her. But how far did he intend to go?

As Bryant kissed her, Lilly wondered what she should do. Should she protest? Should she wait and see what happened? She wondered if Bobby would come looking for her now that her shift was almost over. She looked at the wooden door in the background hoping a knock would come.

It didn't.

Suddenly, she felt Bryant's fingers grope her thighs and move upwards. Her heart started racing. His hands quickly slid across her back and her chest and then his fingers slipped down the front of her dress, below her waist. She protested.

"I need to go," she said, getting upset, trying to push him away.

Then, trying to escape his grasp, Lilly moved toward the door. Bryant immediately stepped in front of her and blocked her path.

She told others later that Bryant seemed to act as if his advances were an honor to be appreciated. Then, to her astonishment, the 6-foot-7-inch athlete extended his hand around her neck and began to squeeze. As she gasped for air, she began to tremble. Her mouth began to quake and she could feel her teeth begin to chatter as Bryant's grip tightened. She tried to pry his hand from her neck, but he was too powerful.

Slowly, Bryant turned her around while keeping a tight grip on her neck. As he walked, he pushed her across the room to the chair he had been sitting on. Controlling her movements, Bryant then bent her over the chair. Using his free hand, he lifted up her black skirt.

"I need to leave," Lilly sobbed, beginning to see starbursts. "No," she said.

She was terrified. Was this really happening? Didn't he understand? She wanted to leave. She wanted to clock out and go home.

Bryant then pulled off her panties.

"No!" she shouted. And then suddenly, pain. As she began crying, she said nothing.

As Bryant went inside of her, she heard him say, *"Yeah, I like Colorado."*

As he pushed her face down into the chair, Lilly felt a tear fall from her cheek and onto her lower lip, which she was now biting. She wanted it to be over.

In the background, she could hear Bryant moaning.

Then, she could feel him lean closer. As he spoke, she could feel his breath in her ear.

*"Do you like it when guys come in your face?"*

"No!" she screamed.

Moments later he was done and allowed his hand to be pulled from her neck. She could feel him back away.

*"Kiss my cock,"* Bryant said.

"No," she said.

At that, he leaned forward and pulled her head toward him and made her do what he demanded—and what she had refused. As soon as she was able, Lilly stood up, horrified at herself and the circumstances.

"You're not going to tell anyone about this . . . are you?" he asked.

Shaking, she quietly uttered, "No."

*"Say it louder,"* Bryant demanded.

"No!" she said, terrified of the consequence of disobedience.

Then she began crying. Annoyed, Bryant rolled his eyes.

"Clean yourself up in the bathroom," he ordered. As she tried to collect herself, Bryant became more specific.

"Fix your hair and wipe your eyes," he said firmly.

[In the October 13, 2003 issue of *Newsweek*, reporter Allison Samuels revealed that Bryant had told friends that in an attempt to help her clean up, he had tried to put ice on Lilly's eyes because she had begun to cry hysterically during the encounter.]

When she finally left the room, she walked downstairs in a daze. Once she reached the lobby, she saw Bobby Pietrack sitting on a sofa by the fireplace talking with a Cordillera couple who were regulars. Breathing heavily, she motioned to him, letting him know that something was wrong. Bobby, who was smiling, suddenly frowned and stood up, bidding the guests farewell.

In the distance, Lilly barely noticed the night auditor more than 30 feet away who seemed to be looking around the lobby. She could barely make out the auditor's expression.

Pietrack took Lilly in the back room. She told him she just wanted to go home. As she filled out her closing night report, her hand shook violently. Scribbled and almost illegible, the police would later view the report as the mark of someone under incredible stress.

Finally, as she walked out with Pietrack, he pressed her to talk. Slowly, she told him what happened. As she related the details of her story, his face lost all color.

"I don't understand," she said, shaking her head. "I just don't understand what happened."

Pietrack, who was angry now, nodded his head.

"I do," he said. "I know exactly what happened."

Lilly looked up at him without saying a word. Pietrack took a deep breath.

"*You were raped,*" he finished.

# 11

## "MISS F"

When the Los Angeles Lakers got their first look at Kobe Bryant in Honolulu on October 3, six days before his scheduled preliminary hearing in Colorado, he was not the man they'd last seen four months earlier.

He had become someone else completely in those 100-plus days, the familiar swagger and confident, reassuring smile long gone. It had to be perplexing to the men who'd come to know, as much as he'd allow, this self-possessed, intensely driven athlete.

When the team widely picked to win the league title encamped on the island of Oahu on October 2, with new arrivals Karl Malone and Gary Payton joining the showtime Lakers cast, Bryant's No. 8 was nowhere to be seen. It was disclosed by team officials that he was ill and would be joining the team later.

The following day, Bryant showed up with an entirely new look. Fresh tattoos ran from his left shoulder to his elbow proclaiming his devotion to wife Vanessa, baby daughter Natalia and his Christian faith.

Yet something was missing. First off, about 20 pounds of the most sensational player in the universe were gone. Bryant had fallen to about two hundred pounds without benefit of his customary summer workouts; a regimen strenuous enough to drain an Olympian. One of the more popular Kobe commercials had shown him working out like a madman, boxing, running, training as if his life depended on reaching peak physical condition. It was a rare case of truth in advertising.

In Honolulu, however, he looked frail, drained and oddly vulnerable for an athlete known for his fiercely competitive nature. There was no bounce in his step and no accuracy in his shot. His efforts repeatedly clanged off rims as reporters ringed the court, film crews zeroing in on the man who was more removed from his environment than ever before.

Clearly, he was not right physically. His right knee had been surgically treated in Vail on July 1, the day after the incident that rocked the sports world in nearby Edwards.

The knee, which would be wrapped in ice when he wasn't on the court, was not sound. He'd also had surgery on his right shoulder, injured during the playoffs. Team management had been disturbed that Bryant had gone to Colorado for the knee surgery without their knowledge; now, judging by the limp, there was reason to wonder if he'd be able to perform physically, to say nothing of the immense emotional burden.

Finally, meeting with the media after a few words with Lakers publicity director John Black, Bryant made religious references—something he'd not done in the past—while reaffirming his devotion to his family.

"To be honest with you," Bryant said, "I'd much rather play basketball and not be famous."

That, of course, would not happen anytime soon. The events of June 30, 2003, made certain that Bryant's every move would be chronicled for the balance of his professional life.

"I'd rather do something else that I love doing, getting paid well to do it and being able to be married to my wife and raise our children without anybody bothering us when we go out in public, or everybody scrutinizing every little detail and everybody making up rumors about our lives," Bryant said. "I'll take that rather than this any day."

"Going through something like this humbles you, and you understand that your ultimate purpose here is to do God's work. I'm out there playing basketball . . . . It's just about maximizing the blessing that God has given me. It's not about the money. It's not about the fame and all the other stuff.

"It's about going out there and doing what I do best and having a good time doing it."

Yet, as his team went through its paces around him, the question inevitably surfaced: Would the Lakers actually be better off without the distractions provided by a man widely hailed as the most exciting talent in the game?

Head coach Phil Jackson admitted "it's an added distraction, a kind of pall that hangs over us."

A man with nine NBA titles as a head coach—the next would separate him from Boston legend Red Auerback as the winningest coach ever—Jackson had seen his share of weirdness over the years, notably with Dennis Rodman in Chicago. That team, featuring the incomparable Michael Jordan and Scottie Pippen, was known as the Beatles of the NBA.

But this—CNN camera crew here, Court TV there, FOX looming in a corner—was something new.

"I really can't find anything comparable," the Zen coach said. "I'm certain I look at every year as a great challenge. But this is going to be one of the most challenging years I can see."

Jackson, who had to break Bryant like a stubborn thoroughbred when he came to Los Angeles in 1999, voiced support of his superstar guard while admitting that Kobe was nowhere close to game shape.

"His leg's so weak, he couldn't get a shot to the basket almost for a while," Jackson said after observing Kobe in an early drill. "He fatigued really early in practice."

On the record, Bryant kept a brave front.

"Do I look like I quitter?" Bryant said when someone wondered if he'd considered taking the season off. "I try not to worry about things I can't control. I have faith. And I'm going to fight." The bout of his life would be in a courtroom, not on a court, and would center on his freedom, not a fourth NBA championship.

\* \* \*

Bryant's arrival at the courthouse for the preliminary hearing on October 9 was almost a rerun of his August 7 advisement. Ironically, there were fewer members of the public, and most journalists had already moved inside the building. Bryant stepped out of a sports utility vehicle, once again assisting his female lead attorney Pamela Mackey who was about to make national headlines with an unexpected performance that would baffle reporters around the globe.

After her performance it was widely agreed that if you believed Bryant, Pamela Mackey was a genius. And if you believed the woman, Pamela Mackey was an evil genius.

From the moment she bounced to her feet from the defense table to register her first objection, the preliminary hearing was no longer Kobe's show. It was the Pamela Mackey Show. It was the performance of a lifetime—Kobe Bryant's lifetime—and all he had to do was sit quietly and watch without emotion. The All Star became the bench warmer.

Mackey's objective was simple: Lay the foundation of reasonable doubt. If she had failed, it would have begun a long downward spiral that might end with Bryant being sentenced to prison for life. By almost all accounts, she did not fail.

Right up to the second the preliminary hearing began, almost no one believed Bryant's defense team would go through with it. Televised talking head after talking head, attorney after attorney, insisted Bryant's attorneys, Mackey and Hal Haddon, had nothing to gain by publicly airing, for a curious world, the accusations against client Bryant. Surely, the collected intelligentsia insisted, Pamela Mackey would waive Bryant's right to a preliminary hearing and go straight to trial, where the standard of proof was far higher.

They were wrong.

When the preliminary hearing was finally over, few were discussing the evidence Deputy District Attorney Gregg Crittenden and Eagle County Sheriff's Detective Doug Winters spent more than two hours laying out. They only talked about her, the questions, the bombshells, the sexual habits of Bryant's alleged victim in the days leading up to June 30 and mostly about the way Mackey aired the alleged victim's dirty laundry in public.

In a court of law, evidence is only intended to come from witness testimony. Those who sit in judgment, judges and juries, are supposed to pay no attention to attorneys for either side. Lawyers are meant to be nothing more than the conveyors of the evidence. But in the court of public opinion, from which a jury of Bryant's peers was to be selected to determine his guilt or innocence, no such rules applied.

"The only reason they had this preliminary hearing was to smear the victim," said former Denver District Attorney Norm Early after the prelim was over. "I've never seen anything like this. It was deliberate. It was despicable. It was just sleazy."

It was possibly all that, but it was also brilliant.

A couple months before, Bryant's August advisement was the biggest non-event since Y2K. Still, hundreds of media gathered to chronicle the seven and a half minute affair. His only words were, "No sir," when asked whether he minded if the charges against him and his rights were left unread to an international television audience.

That warm August afternoon saw hundreds more curiosity seekers pack the viewing area outside the courthouse, trying to get a glimpse of Bryant.

They cheered, they jeered, and when the spectacle was over, they left.

But October was different in the Rocky Mountains. It was fall: Beautiful but serious. The day of Bryant's preliminary hearing was Chamber of Commerce weather. The stunning gold aspen leaves stood against the deep blue sky on a perfect autumn day. August 6 was a circus, and the whole thing didn't seem quite real, yet. October 9 was officially autumn, with winter coming on hard and fast. There were no crowds on that day, unless you count the six college students handing out condoms for a new prophylactic company. The package included a legal consent form for all participants to sign, and listed a number of sex acts to check off that all would agree to.

"If Kobe'd had these, we wouldn't have to be here today," said one of the young women passing out the promotional packages. Protect Condoms. Their slogan: "Protect your assets."

The Eagle County Justice Center, the most important court in Kobe Bryant's life at that moment, was an undistinguished gray stone and block building, leaning more toward function than form. To get to Courtroom One, where Eagle County Court Judge Fred Gannett presided, media and spectators had to pass through the only two metal detectors in Eagle County.

A half hour before the preliminary hearing's 1 p.m. start, Deputy Bill Kaufman, wearing a uniform that included bullet proof vest and sidearm, emptied the hallway, ushering the gathered media into one of two courtrooms—Judge Gannett's courtroom where the preliminary hearing would be held, and an auxiliary courtroom two doors down for the overflow crowd.

Kaufman, smiling at the spectacle, arranged everyone into their chairs as the players quietly strode in without eye contact or reactions of any sort.

First the defense: Haddon, then Bryant, then Mackey. Mackey and Bryant looked like an exclamation point, him 6-foot- 7, her a petite 5-foot-5. But there was no mistaking who was in charge. Bryant held her doors, helped her out of the Chevy Suburban and pulled out her chairs. This stage-managed chivalry was portrayed on national television to an unwitting audience. Bryant repeatedly told reporters he had placed his fate and faith in God's hands, but until he stood before God in judgment, his fate and faith were clearly in the hands of Pamela Mackey.

As they sat at the defense table, the 6-foot-3 Haddon sprawled as if he was in his living room, Bryant sat quietly with his hands folded in front of him and his eyes focused straight ahead, and Mackey busily shuffled papers.

The prosecutors then entered, Ingrid Bakke first. She had been brought to the team from the Boulder County district attorney's office, where she specialized in putting rapists in prison. She was tall, striking and serious. Deputy District Attorney Gregg Crittenden was followed by District Attorney Mark Hurlbert.

"All rise," announced Kaufman.

Eagle County Court Judge Fred Gannett entered the room. Under his robe he was wearing his trademark golf vest and red tie. His top shirt button was open. Although the world was watching, he took no special measures to change his appearance. His beard and hair looked the same as they always did: a bit too long and slightly unruly. But he was unconcerned with appearances. As far as he was concerned, the people in his courtroom that day hadn't been there the day before and they wouldn't be there the day after. The judge treated everyone with respect, as long as they reciprocated.

Judge Gannett opened court that day as he did every day, with a few instructions and admonishments, then instructed the prosecution to call its first witness. Deputy Prosecutor Crittenden called Detective Doug Winters to the stand, Gannett swore him in, and the battle was begun.

The detective testified as to what Lilly Fuller had told him when he interviewed her the day after the incident. He recalled that Lilly's shift was supposed to end at 7 p.m., but she stayed late because she wanted to make up the hours, and was excited to meet Kobe Bryant, whom she heard was arriving at the hotel.

About 9:30 p.m., Lilly was telephoned at the hotel by one of Bryant's entourage, who told her that Bryant wanted to be taken straight to his room. He did not want to stop at the front desk to check in. Bryant then arrived at the hotel at about 10 p.m. When Bryant and his two bodyguards arrived, Lilly met them at the front door with Bryant's room key. Lilly took Bryant and his bodyguards straight to Bryant's room without stopping at the front desk, testified Winters.

At Bryant's room, the basketball star quietly pulled Lilly aside and asked her to return to his room later to give him a tour of the property, Winters said.

"He asked it quietly, like he didn't want the other people to hear him," said Winters. "She agreed."

Winters said Lilly told him Bryant's entourage wouldn't let anyone near his room. He said the young woman told him they were also keeping an eye on the lobby.

"She was excited to meet him," said Winters. "She said she was somewhat flattered."

The Lodge and Spa at Cordillera contained 56 rooms. When Bryant and his bodyguards arrived that Monday evening, only four were occupied. Lilly, who made the room assignments, had 52 rooms to choose from.

Lilly put Bryant in Room 35, at the end of the first floor hallway—"as far away from the front desk and lobby area as you could get," Lilly told Winters. None of the other rooms on that hallway were occupied.

Lilly returned to the front desk to pick up the keys for Bryant's bodyguards' rooms at the opposite end of the hotel. Once she had shown them to their rooms, she took a back way to return to Bryant's room. She had to duck out the hotel's front door, back in through the employee entrance, through the employee cafeteria, up a hallway and down an elevator to the first floor to Room 35 where Bryant was waiting.

Lilly knocked on his door, he answered and they started their tour.

"She did indicate he was flirtatious," said Winters. "He was giving her compliments about her appearance, her dress and her height."

Winters said she told him Bryant asked if she had a boyfriend. She said she didn't at the time. Winters said Lilly was flattered by Bryant's attention, and excited he was showing an interest in her.

Eventually they ended up back at Bryant's room and he invited her in.

Winters continued that once inside the room, she made conversation about where the bears would approach the ground floor windows of Bryant's suite, along with other small talk.

Among other things, they talked about a tattoo and Bryant asked her if she wanted a hot tub later. She said "no," and that she wanted to get home. She told Winters that she was beginning to feel uncomfortable with the situation, but that she did not communicate that to Bryant.

Winters continued to testify that as the assault was beginning, "she said he knew she wanted to leave, because she said she kept moving toward the door. When she moved, he'd move in that direction.

"She stated during the interview that she indicated to him that she wanted to leave," said Winters. And that as the assault was taking place, "she said 'No' to him. She said 'No' when he lifted up her skirt.

"It was clear and concise," said Winters of the alleged victim's tone and volume. "I didn't have any trouble understanding her. You could clearly hear her."

Winters said that's when Bryant "proceeded to have sexual intercourse with her." Winters said she told him she said "no" during the intercourse, and that she was upset and started to cry. He said she told him she was in pain, and that she bled.

During Mackey's cross-examination, the defense raised the issue that there was some confusion as to when Lilly said "no," if at all. Winters responded that during the initial interview, he asked Lilly how she communicated to Bryant that she was an unwilling partner in a sexual act.

In his report, Winters indicated he asked Lilly why she never said "No." When asked the question during cross-examination, Winters said the woman did not "protest," or indicate that she had said, "No."

Winters said Lilly testified that Bryant finally stopped when she pried his hand from around her throat.

"So when she pulled his hand from her throat, he stopped. Is that correct, Detective?" Mackey asked Winters, implying that move was the first sign of a "no" from Lilly, and that Bryant had clearly complied.

"That's correct," said Winters.

Winters testified that Lilly said she was in Bryant's room about five minutes. Winters added that she told him that when the sexual intercourse was finished, "he asked if she was going to say anything about it, and she said 'No,' but that she said 'No' because she feared retribution or physical harm."

Winters finished the prosecution's portion of the hearing with, "She said she had no intention of having sexual intercourse with Mr. Bryant."

During the defense's cross-examination, Winters testified he had not seen any bruising on the alleged victim's throat. He said the first bruising he had seen was in a photograph provided by the Sexual Assault Nurse Examiners, who examined both Lilly and Bryant.

Mackey said the only bruise on the alleged victim was on her left jaw and it was about half the size of a penny.

Mackey also pointed out the alleged victim's vaginal injuries did not need stitches or even a topical ointment. She objected to two photographs being introduced into evidence that the nurse examiners said depicted the alleged victim's larger vaginal lacerations.

Those images were magnified, and the injuries were treated with a blue dye to make them easier to see.

Testimony during Mackey's cross-examination indicated that there was bilateral redness but no trauma was observed to the labia majora, no cuts, tears or lacerations to the labia minora, no trauma was observed to the vagina, clitoris and hymen. Redness was observed to the cervix, and no trauma was observed to the rectum.

According to the nurses' reports, the only medications the alleged victim received were for the prevention of sexually transmitted diseases, Mackey asserted during cross-examination.

Winters said Lilly admitted having sexual intercourse on June 28 and that her partner had used a condom. Winters added that according to the nurses' reports and photos, the injuries were not consistent with consensual sex, but with penetrating genital trauma. The detective testified that the nurse examiners told him the injuries Lilly suffered were likely not caused by consensual sex during the last two or three days prior to June 30. He said they told him the injuries had occurred within the past 24 hours of her rape examination on July 1.

When the detective questioned Bryant the next night, Bryant was wearing the same T-shirt he wore the night before but Bryant had it tucked into his sweat pants, so Winters didn't notice the blood stains on it. It was later revealed that there were three such stains matching the DNA of Bryant's alleged victim.

Dozens of times during Crittenden's questioning, Mackey bounced to her feet to object to the prosecution's supposed leading questions to Winters. Bryant, meanwhile, sat motionless, expressionless, and with his hands folded on the table before him.

As Crittenden and Winters were laying out their case, the details became increasingly graphic. In the few moments that Mackey was not objecting to one of Crittenden's questions, she was making Bryant look less the monster that he was being described as. As the prosecution Q&A began describing the genital trauma and tears Bryant had allegedly caused, Mackey placed her hand gently in the middle of Bryant's back and pulled him to her, leaning over and whispering in his ear as if to tell the crowd gathered behind, *He's not intimidating at all. He's scared, just like you would be.*

As the afternoon wore on, observers quit looking at Bryant. He was not the star of his own show. During the two hours Crittenden and Winters laid out the prosecution's case, Mackey continually objected and Judge Gannett often sustained them. At one point, Judge Gannett wondered aloud if Crittenden's law school evidence classes had used the same definitions the judge's had, prompting numerous spectators to chuckle.

Then, when Crittenden asked Winters what happened after "he raped her," Mackey objected.

"Your honor, something is going to have to be done about these leading questions," she said.

Crittenden, who looked at his colleagues puzzled, turned to Gannett and responded, "Your honor, I don't think 'what happened next' is a leading question."

Again, the courtroom tried to suppress its laughter.

Still, the evidence the prosecution laid out should have been damning.

But an hour later, after defense attorney Pamela Mackey was through, no one was talking about any of that: not the way Bryant sneaked away from his bodyguards to pull Lilly aside and privately ask her to return to his room, not the alleged rape, not her blood on Bryant's T-shirt and her underwear.

All anyone could talk about was how, as her cross examination of Winters began, Mackey blurted out Lilly's name six times in open court—unheard of in a rape case—how the crowded courtroom audibly gasped, how Mackey seemed genuinely surprised to hear the name come out of her own mouth.

The first time, Mackey said it as if in passing. It sounded like an honest mistake. In the middle of a sentence that she quickly and quietly uttered, the name "Lilly Fuller" seemed to naturally roll off her tongue. Then it happened again—and again. Finally, Crittenden pointed out the "mistakes" to the judge who halted the hearing and told the courtroom that everyone would have to make a stronger effort not to use the alleged victim's name.

Mackey apologized and continued. Almost instantly she amplified her voice while pressing the detective and said "Lilly Fuller." Journalists in the courtroom looked at one another, confused. What was Mackey up to? It didn't seem to make sense. Everyone in the press seemed to agree this was no mistake—but why? Couldn't she tell this was a public relations disaster?

After the sixth time, Mackey told Gannett that it was going to be very difficult for her not to use the alleged victim's name. As an alternative, Mackey suggested she call the alleged victim by another name. Gannett, who seemed annoyed, simply responded, "Or maybe I could just get out the muzzle." The spectators laughed, nodding in agreement.

Mackey herself played down the comment with a light laugh and repeated her request, which Gannett granted.

Apparently, the judge didn't catch on to the innuendo that most of the press did—that Mackey's new name, "Miss F," was a thinly veiled reference at profanity. Later, when reporters discussed Mackey's courtroom behavior, they agreed that Mackey's strong enunciation of the letter "F," implied that it stood for something other than the alleged victim's last name.

Mackey followed the name uproar with a 20-minute line of questioning designed to surgically slice open the prosecution's case. Mackey revealed that the room above Bryant's was occupied on the night in question and that the guests had slept with their windows open. She reported that the guests claimed to have heard nothing.

Mackey reminded the court that when the couple reached Bryant's room and went inside, Lilly later told Winters that she expected Bryant to "put a move on her." [Later, when Lilly heard Winters' statement, she became annoyed. The young concierge clarified to a small group of friends that she had expected Bryant to continue with his flirtations, but that she didn't expect him to make a physical move on her—regardless of how it sounded in court.]

Mackey then asserted that Lilly's injuries weren't actually injuries at all. Even if they were, she explained, they certainly didn't support an accusation like the one Lilly, the sheriff and the district attorney were making.

There were no bruises on the body, back, legs, arms or wrists, Mackey led Detective Winters to admit during cross-examination. Both the victim and the accuser each submitted to rape examination at Valley View Hospital in Glenwood Springs. Those exams turned up no signs of a struggle, not on Lilly's body or on Bryant's.

The vaginal injuries couldn't be explained or even recognized without the Sexual Assault Nurse Examiners report, Mackey again had Winters admit. The photos of the supposed vaginal injuries were magnified and treated with a blue dye to make the injuries stand out. They were apparently difficult for Winters to decipher.

As Mackey questioned Winters, she fired off the line of the day when she asked, "Where's the vagina, Detective Winters?"

As Winters looked from the photographs to Mackey and back, he smiled sheepishly and said, "I'm not sure."

The courtroom crowd gasped and tittered. Judge Gannett's head jerked up from the copious notes he was taking as he peered out across the crowd and shot Mackey his best, "we are not amused" look.

"That was not meant to be funny," she said.

But it was funny, in a sad way. And it was at that point, at that moment, that the focus shifted. The prosecution's only witness in the preliminary hearing, a law-enforcement veteran, couldn't find the vagina in a blown-up photograph that was meant to help convince a judge to put one of America's most popular athletes, a modern day marketing machine, on trial for rape.

Right then, the focus shifted. And like Mackey's question, the shift was not subtle. Nor was the question that quickly followed. When she led Winters to answer a question about the nature of the injuries—two lacerations, each one centimeter long and several others one millimeter long—Winters responded that the nurse examiners told him Lilly's injuries were consistent with penetrating genital trauma; they were not consistent with consensual sex.

"Could they be consistent with someone who has had sex with three men in three days?" Mackey asked.

As the audible wheeze from the crowd could be heard in the hallway outside, prosecutor Ingrid Bakke jumped up from the third chair at the prosecutor's table to object. As she did, she pushed her left hand into the middle of Crittenden's back to get him out of his chair. He leaped to his feet.

Judge Gannett brought the entire proceeding to a screeching halt and cleared his courtroom in a flash.

The judge ordered attorneys for both sides into his chambers for what was described in the media as a "severe chewing out," while reporters scrambled for the only payphone in the Eagle County courthouse to call their editors (their cell phones and laptops had been confiscated at the metal detectors). When one woman stayed on the phone too long, another reporter walked to the phone and hung it up. The offended reporter became furious and began shouting.

Television correspondents dashed outside to their broadcast platforms and tents, to relay to their viewing public what they'd just heard. They didn't look into television cameras and breathlessly summarize the two hours the prosecution had spent presenting their evidence. The majority of them simply spit out the question Mackey had asked Winters: Could it be that Lilly's injuries were caused by having sex with three men in three days?

Gannett kept the attorneys out for an hour and 20 minutes. Plenty of time for everyone to use the payphone and plenty of time for television's talking heads to ask each other the question over and over, analyze what they thought it meant, and whether or not Mackey did it on purpose.

In one more example of the spin wars, former Denver Deputy Prosecutor Craig Silverman reported that blurting out Lilly's name six times in court was an accident. Among those confused as to Silverman's comments was former Denver prosecutor Norm Early, who told another television camera, "Nothing Pamela Mackey does in court is an accident. You don't say the victim's name six times in open court, then follow it with that question, and call it an accident. It was intentional. It was despicable. This is why so many women fear reporting rape. They don't want to go through what this woman is going through."

What Early didn't know was that Silverman had been on the payroll of the tabloids in the past. Silverman's relationship with the Denver legal community had become invaluable to the tabloids, which frequently quoted him as an expert or source close to the investigation. During the JonBenet Ramsey murder case, *Globe* editors in need of attributing a story or a quote to a "source" would frequently call Silverman for help.

Some people suspected that Silverman had a professional relationship of some sort with Bryant's defense team, but the allegation was never proved. Others assumed that Silverman was just bucking for support from the Denver firm that he knew could be a powerful ally for him in the future as he was considering running for public office. One way or another, Silverman's comments, which constantly came to the defense of Bryant's lawyers, mystified his fellow prosecutors and more than a few journalists.

[In an October issue of the *Globe*, Silverman inferred that it was possible Lilly had lied to police about her allegations that Bryant raped her.

"Rape is an abomination—so is a false accusation of rape. I'm all for victim's rights. But I'm trying to figure out who the victim is here."]

While Silverman was chatting up the journalists, some reporters tried speaking with Bryant's security men. One of the security men had allegedly contacted a friend of Lilly Fuller and identified himself as an investigator with the Los Angeles Police Department. The friend, who was working for a national television news network as a runner, told her supervisors who in turn reported the matter to the Eagle County Sheriff's Department who tried to organize a sting for the man, to no avail.

On the opposite side of the courtroom, John Clune, a lawyer for Lilly Fuller who used to work as the former Eagle County Chief Deputy Prosecutor, stared out the glass doors toward the mountains. The former prosecutor was extremely disappointed in the defense team's decision to stoop to the low level of using his client's real name in court. As Clune tried isolating himself from the dozens of reporters that encircled him, Judge Gannett called the preliminary hearing back to order.

The break had lasted 80 minutes. At 6:20 p.m., the judge said he'd had enough for one day and recessed until the following Wednesday. And so it was that "The Question" entered the court of public opinion.

"Once that bell is rung, you can't unring it," said Bakke.

Norm Early told reporters that he was shocked Kobe Bryant's defense attorneys would resort to smear tactics. He said Mackey put the question out there when she did hoping the public would hear it. When it brought the proceedings to a screeching halt, it was the last thing people in the courtroom heard, and its echo resonated in print and on television talk shows for five days.

"The defense hopes the public will hear that, because out of the public will come the 12 jurors who will decide this case," said Early. "This woman is suffering what every woman fears in a rape case. No one thought the defense would stoop this low."

# 12

## THE SHIFTING SANDS

Bryant's defense attorney's literally and figuratively aired Lilly Fuller's dirty laundry in public, slipping innuendo (and not subtle at that) about her recent sexual history through a tiny loophole in the rape shield law. That law prohibits discussion of an alleged victim's sexual history during a trial. It does not specifically mention the preliminary hearing, so if it was to come up, it had to come up at the preliminary hearing.

In his career, District Attorney Mark Hurlbert had specialized in the placement of blame.

As the tumultuous first half of Bryant's preliminary hearing swirled around him, Hurlbert sat in the first chair of the prosecution table, quiet and motionless.

"There is more to this case," he said, "much more."

Assertions from Bryant's defense attorneys that the alleged victim had sex with three men in three days was certainly an atom bomb when it was dropped, but when the point-counterpoint people began breaking through with the basic fact that it didn't have anything to do with the issue at hand, that Kobe Bryant allegedly raped Lilly Fuller that night, and that the law says no other nights matter, the story's pace slowed to a crawl. The biggest bomb was yet to come.

From the beginning of the entire process in early July, an informational black hole had existed in the case into which Bryant's defense team threw the media-beast something to chew on every few days. The frenzy began anew when, during what amounted to the preliminary hearing halftime (lasting Friday through Tuesday), retired District Court Judge William Jones held forth for a couple New York journalists in Eagle covering the hearing. The judge passed along information he told them he got from Bryant's co-defense counsel, Hal Haddon. This was perceived by many to be a huge breach of the very specific gag-order that was issued by the judge intended to keep the attorney's from both sides from saying anything to anyone about the case.

As a result of the rather gargantuan leak, on October 11, the *New York Daily News* reported that the alleged victim had another man's semen in her underwear when she showed up for her rape test. The country was stunned. What type of person was this woman? It was altogether mind-boggling.

One of the local print reporters led a television crew up to a tiny mining enclave high in the mountains surrounding Eagle, where Jones had a cabin. He wasn't there, or anywhere else anyone was looking.

Jones told the *New York Daily News* he and Haddon had known each other for about 40 years, and that Haddon was doing some work for him.

Hurlbert had had about enough. First the ambush that blew up the first half of the preliminary hearing, and then the ill-disguised leak. A column in the *Vail Daily* testily alluded to Haddon leaking information to Jones. Haddon immediately fired off an e-mail to *Vail Daily* Managing Editor Don Rogers insisting he hadn't talked to Jones in ten years.

District attorney's investigator Gerry Sandberg finally cornered Jones to ask him a few questions. Jones said he hadn't talked to Haddon in ten years. If they didn't talk to each other, who did? That's what Hurlbert wanted to know.

Hurlbert pointed out that when Jones talked to the *Daily News*, the first half of the preliminary hearing had been conducted and the information had not been presented as evidence. The district attorney accused Bryant's attorneys of campaigning to get information to the public that had been sealed by the court. He said Mackey and Haddon were disregarding the court's orders limiting pretrial publicity, culminating with the Jones leak.

"Given that few people knew the information before the second part of the preliminary hearing, Jones does not appear to be telling the truth," said Hurlbert.

Hurlbert asked the judge for an independent investigation of the defense tactics. "Since Jones is being untruthful, maybe an independent agency may be able to get him closer to the truth," said Hurlbert.

Haddon wasn't talking. The judge had disappeared. There was no way to confirm any of it. The story died down and everyone waited for Wednesday.

\* \* \*

When Kobe Bryant's day in court resumed, everyone expected Pamela Mackey's grilling of Detective Doug Winters to pick up right where it had left off, solving the three-guys-in-three-days mystery. In contrast to the theatrics of the previous Thursday, Mackey's second-half performance was methodical and calculated.

She acted like the question had never been raised and launched straight into questions about the mystery semen, hammering at Winters about why he hadn't tested to find out whose it was. Mackey was headed down a time-tested road traveled by successful rape defense attorneys: shift the spotlight from the accused to the accuser. Put the victim on trial; make her out to be a "nut or a slut," or ideally, both. In addition, no one was even thinking about Bryant, which was just how she wanted it. They were thinking instead about Miss Pamela Mackey. At one point, Mackey even introduced testimony from the night-auditor Trina McKay, who was sitting 30 feet away, that asserted that Lilly's demeanor was not consistent with someone who had undergone a traumatic experience. What was not revealed however, was that McKay, according to sources, had spent a significant portion of the evening of June 30 chatting with Bryant in the lobby. In addition, several days later McKay told police investigators that Lilly "must be making the whole thing up." When confronted by a reporter about her accusation of the young concierge, McKay denied the charge despite the police reports indicating otherwise.

Through it all, Hurlbert sat quietly, almost stoic. He was like a teenager behind the wheel of a hotrod. He couldn't wait to step on the gas. But not yet.

The semen certainly existed, but it might as well not have. The prosecution didn't test it because they believed it to be irrelevant. It didn't matter; Hurlbert and his investigators had known about it since early July, before Bryant was ever charged. They knew about the semen, the sexual history allegations, the two overdoses and everything else that would pop up as the months wore on and the trial grew closer. Knowing all that, they charged Bryant anyway.

When Bryant's preliminary hearing was over and the collected wisdom of the nation's media was dismissing the DA's case as weak and misguided, Hurlbert simply responded that no prosecutor presents his entire case at a preliminary hearing.

And, not surprisingly, the nation seemed to be divided along ethnic lines as well. When asked about the case on popular cable television show *Tough Crowd with Colin*

*Quinn,* a New York comedian said, "It's hard to imagine a white guy accused of raping a black girl getting standing ovations and cheers as he toured the country," in reference to the reception afforded Bryant as he and his Lakers began the 2003-04 season.

Shortly after the preliminary hearing, the Eagle County Sheriff's Office printed 76 T-shirts that read, "Hang Kobe," with the picture of a stick-man dangling from a noose. Although the move was meant as a joke, Pamela Mackey would later consider using it as evidence that there was the specter of racism haunting the department and the area. To further bolster her claim, the National Alliance, a virulent neo-Nazi organization, had littered the town of Eagle with racist flyers in August accusing African-American men of trying to poison white women with the AIDS virus. Although the flyers were later found in neighboring counties as well, it would surely prompt questions among Bryant's defense that perhaps Eagle County was not among the more racially diverse counties to hold a fair trial.

Famous talk-show host Montel Williams, when asked about the case said, "I served in the US Navy so I could defend the Constitution of the United States and the premise that you are innocent until proven guilty. This case is sickening. This guy has already been convicted in the media. Who cares what happens at trial? The guy's already been found guilty."

# 13

## FRONT AND CENTER

Mark Hurlbert was a Nordic skier and ultra-long distance runner. He skied on the Nordic team at Dartmouth. Earlier in the summer of 2003 he was part of a team that ran in a charity event from Georgetown to Glenwood Springs, more than one hundred miles over two mountain passes. The event was long, grueling and had huge ups and downs. Life was like that. So was law.

Beginning at the crack of dawn, the Saturday after he charged Bryant as a felon rapist, the Eagle County District Attorney smiled at television camera after television camera, microphone after microphone, reporter after reporter.

He understood that the journalists were simply doing their job as he answered the same questions over and over:

"What did you know and when did you know it?"

"What did you do and why did you do it?"

In a busy summer for major news stories, Hurlbert was in the eye of the biggest media storm of all.

Besides the television cameras and reporters, Hurlbert faced an opposition with millions of dollars to throw at the case, and the combined marketing forces of hundreds of people who made a very good living from the Kobe Bean Bryant Industry, and who weren't about to let their gravy train be derailed without a fight.

"We're doing fine," Hurlbert said when asked how he was holding up. "We're ready to get on with the next phase."

He politely thanked people who asked how Lilly was. Hurlbert made the rounds, building his case for both the court of law and the court of public opinion. Between July 19 and July 21, he was on television more than he was at home. He charmed and disarmed. Questions about the evidence or the investigation were met with a slight nod of the head and a smiling, "I can't comment on that." Those questions came by the thousands. He never slipped. Every question was a new opportunity to make a mistake. He understood this.

Hurlbert's investigators collected their evidence. He examined it thoroughly and conferred with prosecutors all over Colorado, gathering opinions and advice from people he respected. He knew, though, that the decision to charge Bryant was his alone. He came to that decision on Thursday morning, July 17. He gave the alleged victim and her family a day's advance notice, as he had promised.

On Friday, July 18, he once again stepped into the spotlight and told the world that he had enough evidence to convict Bryant, beyond a reasonable doubt, of what used to be called "forcible rape." To make that case, there had to be sexual contact—penetration—and there had to be violence or the threat of violence. Hurlbert wouldn't comment on the evidence, but nodded and smiled and said, "It appears I can prove my case beyond a reasonable doubt."

He said there was no smoking gun, no single bit of evidence that tipped the scales of justice toward felony charges against Bryant. In weighing evidence, the sum was greater than it's individual parts.

It wasn't the first time Hurlbert had been front and center for the international media. In March, a skier death case put Hurlbert in front of the cameras.

Following a collision at Breckenridge Ski Resort that killed a 56-year-old man from Illinois, Hurlbert had to decide whether or not to file charges against the other man in the crash, Englishman Robert Wills. The case attracted a flurry of international attention. Reporters from the BBC, several London newspapers and periodicals from throughout the United States inquired about details of the accident and a possible court case, forcing Summit County authorities to change messages on voice-mail systems to deal with increased calls. *The New York Times* carried the story of Wills' arrest.

Hurlbert concluded there was not enough evidence to indicate Wills was negligent or out of control, so he dropped the case. Wills' defense attorney was Pamela Mackey.

Media attention was a side of the job he hadn't planned on.

"This wasn't what I was thinking about in law school," Hurlbert said. "The [public relations] side of the job was unexpected."

The television talking heads and newspaper columnists opined that his case was weak, and falling apart. In celebrity cases, the court of public opinion is the foundation for the court of law. The Bryant defense attorneys certainly understood that. Hurlbert's worthy adversary was playing the media like a wily veteran, dropping bits of information into the public consciousness, sending ripples through the potential jury pool. Mackey knew the media would do most of the dirty work, and it did. It was the media that launched the stories about a breakup with a boyfriend, Lilly's two drug overdoses, about her best friend dying in an automobile accident a day before that second overdose, about her rock solid singing performance at her best friend's funeral a few days later, about the trip to Austin, Tex., with a friend for an audition on the television show *American Idol*.

But there was more. At the preliminary hearing, Hurlbert had been ready to present Lilly's videotaped statement, tearfully detailing what she says Bryant did to her. Hurlbert was ready to present as evidence an audiotape Winters recorded when he first questioned Bryant on July 1, the night after the incident.

Judge Gannett said neither was necessary for the preliminary hearing, and would prejudice potential jurors. Hurlbert decided not to push it. For the preliminary hearing he settled for Crittenden questioning Winters. The two would summarize enough evidence to convince Judge Gannett to send Bryant to trial.

Judge Gannett did order Bryant to stand trial, but chided prosecutors for presenting "a minimal amount of evidence." Gannett did say that what evidence prosecutors did show suggested "submission and force." Hurlbert said he remained confident in his case. Mackey said she was disappointed in Judge Gannett's ruling, but was ready to go to trial.

In his ruling, Gannett said he wasn't overwhelmed with the prosecution's evidence. He wrote that if the law had not required him to view the evidence in a light most favorable to the prosecution, there might not be a trial at all. However, some familiar with the relationship between the judge and the D.A. said this was indicative of the strained relationship between the two.

"The People presented, despite the Court's consistent comments and admonitions concerning the amount and the nature of the evidence to be presented at the preliminary hearing, what can only be described as a minimal amount of evidence, relying substantially on the use of hearsay evidence," wrote Gannett.

However, for Gannett, there was no getting away from Lilly's blood on Bryant's T-shirt and her underwear. And that was enough to send Bryant to trial. Gannett was careful to say that a preliminary hearing was not a gauge of a defendant's guilt or innocence—just a determination that, in this case, a sexual assault had likely been committed and that Bryant could have committed it.

The criticism stung from both the media and Gannett's court. One local attorney speculated that Gannett had just been "grandstanding," trying to win attention in his last 15 minutes of face time. District attorney's office investigator Gerry Sandberg dismissed it.

"No one has heard the complete story, yet," said Sandberg.

Sandberg played college football, and knew a couple things to be true, both on the gridiron and in the courtroom.

"Don't try to run with the ball while it's still bouncing," he said.

# 14

## A MAN APART

Of all the road trips in his life, none had compared with this one. Kobe Bryant was used to being alone—just not this alone.

Completely drained, Bryant returned home to Southern California from the preliminary hearing in Eagle County, Colorado, dazed by the dizzying series of events, the legal maneuverings, the uncertainties, the posturing, the inability to control anything.

This was the hardest part, this sense of helplessness. Bryant had always been able to fix flaws in his game with his work ethic. This was different. It was all up to the earnest woman he'd put in charge of his fate, Pamela Mackey, and the legal elite working with her. Bryant would be free of Eagle until November 13, when he was scheduled to reappear for his trial date.

Getting back with his team, starting the long process of whipping his body back into game shape, Bryant wouldn't share in the brand of easy, joking camaraderie with teammates most players would embrace in such difficult circumstances. He'd always set himself apart from them, and that hadn't changed throughout his ordeal. Even though they'd been in his company for nine months a year, over the past seven years, Shaquille O'Neal, Rick Fox and Derek Fisher, his longest standing teammates, were not buddies. Kobe always went his own way. That's just how it was. Nobody even questioned it any more.

Trying to change that, now that Bryant needed all the support he could gather, would feel unnatural, forced. The tattoos were one thing but those didn't talk back or take offense at being used when convenient. The human dynamic had to flow in the normal course of events.

Through most of his professional career, Bryant did have one friend to lean on when things got tough: former Lakers general manager Jerry West, the basketball genius who brought Kobe to L.A. in the summer of 1996 in a draft deal that sent veteran center Vlade Divac to the Charlotte Hornets.

It was seen as a huge gamble at the time—Divac was among the ten best big men in the game while Bryant was a complete unknown—but it served the dual purpose of fortifying the Lakers with Bryant, an outside presence, and O'Neal, the game's dominant inside force. By removing Divac, the Lakers were able to clear enough space from the salary cap to pursue O'Neal, a free agent in Orlando that summer.

West immediately took young Kobe under his wing, sensing a kindred spirit, and remained close with Bryant. But after the 1999-2000 season, the Lakers' legendary leader, emotionally spent, stepped aside for his protege, Mitch Kupchak.

West resurfaced for the 2002-03 season in Memphis, determined to lead the sad-sack Grizzlies to respectability. Though they remained in contact, West and Bryant no longer had the daily relationship that had helped ease the young athlete through a variety of personal and professional storms.

What's more, Kobe's parents, Joe and Pamela, began to have diminishing roles as the marriage with Vanessa became, quite understandably, the focal point of the player's life.

Though known as a master motivator of athletes, Phil Jackson, the Lakers' high-profile coach, never connected on a personal level with Bryant, failing to break through Kobe's hard, protective shell. Bryant respected Jackson's success but wasn't willing to let Phil get inside his head and achieve the kind of closeness the coach had created with Michael Jordan in Chicago.

The relationship between Shaq and Kobe had been complex from the start, two huge egos often finding themselves in conflict over ownership of the ball and the team. There was also the matter of endorsement dollars. Bryant soon emerged as a major player in that arena, hooking deals with heavyweights while causing a certain discontent in the O'Neal camp, which felt the upstart hadn't earned that level of commercial respect with his performance.

Over the years, Shaq and Kobe managed to work out their differences, coming to understand that they would never celebrate championships together until they found common ground on the court. When that happened, in the 1999-2000 season, they appeared to come closer together off the court as well. But that delicate rapport was ruptured again the following season, when Bryant demanded a larger role in the offense and O'Neal, with the support of Jackson, resisted. Again, they worked it out, largely because Kobe submerged his ego when it mattered most. When the Lakers stormed through the playoffs losing only one game, Shaq and Kobe finally appeared to be a real team within the team.

A breakthrough occurred during the Western Conference finals that summer—a sweep of San Antonio. It was triggered by Bryant's finest performance yet in Game 1 when he erupted for 45 points, destroying the Twin Towers of Tim Duncan and David Robinson.

After that game, O'Neal passed Bryant's locker at the Alamodome and extended his right hand in the players' salute of the moment. Tapping fists with Bryant, Shaq leaned over and softly said, "You're my idol, bro." A few minutes later, in the press room, O'Neal said Kobe was the "best player in the league . . . by far." He then expanded that to include "all nine planets."

This was what the rest of the league feared most, that O'Neal and Bryant would work out their differences and form an unbeatable alliance. That fear was confirmed the following season as the Lakers won their third straight title with Shaq and Kobe aligned together, their "Star Wars" combat of the past long forgotten.

It was Jerry West who, behind the scenes, had orchestrated all of this. He pulled Bryant aside to drive home the point that Kobe needed to trust his teammates to become a true champion. This ran against Bryant's basic instinct to control any situation with his individual greatness, in the fashion of Michael Jordan. When he finally saw the light and began to involve teammates on a regular basis, Bryant became the best all-around player in the game. O'Neal was right. Kobe was the best on all nine planets, as far as anyone could determine.

The championship run ended in 2003, largely because O'Neal never worked himself back into dominant form after undergoing toe surgery at the start of the season. Forced to carry the heavy load he'd always wanted, Bryant averaged a career-high 30 points, becoming only the third Laker in history to reach that plateau.

In the playoffs, however, Bryant suffered a shoulder injury going to the hoop in the first round against Minnesota. That, along with a condition in the right knee that would keep him more grounded than usual, cut into Kobe's effectiveness just enough to prevent him from destroying San Antonio again, as he had in previous seasons.

For all the ground he'd covered with his celebrated teammate, Shaq, Bryant remained, at heart, a loner. On the road, he kept to himself, emerging only occasionally and never without his bodyguards. He made it clear that his life was Vanessa and his new baby. Approached by women indiscreetly on the road, Kobe was known to flash them his wedding ring. It was his way of announcing that he was taken.

But now, in the summer of 2003, the whole world knew he'd strayed, cheated on Vanessa, turning his carefully orchestrated life upside down and inside out with one terrible decision in Room 35 at the Lodge and Spa at Cordillera, more than a mile high in the Rockies.

And that, along with the uncertainty of his future, was why Bryant felt lonesome coming back to Southern California after his preliminary hearing.

His teammates, favored to win the championship again with the arrivals of future Hall of Famers Karl Malone and Gary Payton, voiced their support through the media. But Bryant, as always, was a man apart. His commitment now was to getting himself healthy, to regain strength in the knee. And he was getting better by the day, physically at least.

After it was announced by Eagle County Judge Frederick Gannett on October 20, eight days before the season would open, that Bryant would be bound over for trial, the Lakers accepted it with measured nonchalance.

"I thought it was pretty anticlimactic in that it didn't seem to be on the minds of everyone, at least as much as I thought it would be," veteran forward Rick Fox said. "That's including Kobe. Kobe was going through practice as if it was just another day. He's said it before, that he's done what he can do and now he has to let it play out. As far as going to trial, I don't think it was anything anyone didn't expect."

His back against a wall at the Lakers' training facility, Bryant fielded one stray inquiry about the courtroom from a local television producer who had her credential lifted for not obeying club policy to keep all interviews in the basketball arena.

"What courthouse?" Bryant replied, managing a thin smile.

Another question about anxiety evoked a response.

"Basketball? Basketball, zero anxiety," he said. "Other stuff? Ah, a little anxiety. I pretty much give it up. I've pretty much done all I can here. Just, God will carry me the rest of the way. I'm pretty comfortable with that. You do that, you have no problem whatsoever.

"When I play in the games, I don't think about anything else but the game. Come to work, do your job. I love playing basketball. I love my job. I'm thankful for that."

Jackson, noting that all he knew was what he read in the newspapers, alluded to Bryant's next court date—a November 13 hearing in which he'd be advised of the charge, the possible penalties and his rights—and said, "We have no feel at all for where the case is heading."

Jackson was busy trying to get all the new parts of his dream team functioning smoothly. It didn't help that Bryant, the lethal weapon from the perimeter, had not been able to practice with the new men, Payton and Malone. The coach did express satisfaction with Bryant's conditioning and weight training, saying, "He's doing double time right now; that's good. We're pleased."

Yet there remained the issue of a monumental distraction carrying through the entire marathon of a season, fraying nerves along the way.

"I just have to say we want this thing to go as quickly as possible and disappear into thin air," Jackson said, knowing what an impossible dream that was. "That's what we really want it to do, and have a season that's unfettered."

This would be the most fettered of Lakers seasons, without a doubt.

When it was announced that Bryant would make his preseason debut on October 23 in Anaheim against the Los

Angeles Clippers, all available seats in the cavernous Arrowhead Pond, home of the Anaheim Mighty Ducks, were snapped up quickly.

It was a loud and overwhelmingly supportive crowd on game night, not surprising given Bryant's immense popularity and the abiding presumption of innocence in the region. Among those in the crowd were Vanessa Bryant, seated courtside, Bryant's blue-suited bodyguards and Mike Tyson, replete with distinctive facial tattoo.

Tyson, former heavyweight champion and convicted rapist, said he came as a guest of Lakers owner Jerry Buss, with whom the fighter shared a few words.

"I'm just here to watch the game," said Tyson, who, the media was left to conclude, had not come to give Bryant advice on how to handle rape trials.

It was clear the majority of the 18,298 fans were there to offer verbal and visual support, from the countless gold number 8 Bryant jerseys, to the frequent "Ko-be" chants.

The familiar adulation started with a standing ovation when Bryant was introduced with the starting lineup and continued throughout a game won by the Clippers, 107-101. Bryant scored 15 points in 32 minutes, playing with visible energy and emotion. At the finish, the Lakers' star slapped hands and backs with rival Clippers, who reciprocated.

"The crowd support means a lot," Bryant said. "Standing behind me and my family, it meant a lot. I could feel it. I could feel the electricity, the buzz."

He could also feel the rust on his jump shot, missing ten of 14 shots. But that was to be expected from a man playing competitively for the first time in five months, with a surgically repaired right knee and right shoulder.

"It was good to see him back out there, in the flow and smiling," said Malone, second among all-time NBA scorers.

Vanessa Bryant appeared to enjoy the show along with the fans, many of whom were young children wearing

Bryant's No. 8 jersey, the NBA's best seller the previous season. Mrs. Bryant clapped and smiled when her husband made one of his spectacular moves.

"It felt good to be out there and just to play," Bryant said. "It's not going to take away from what I'm going through, but it was enjoyable.

"Am I happy today? I guess you could say so, under the circumstances."

The last thing the Lakers needed—a rekindling of the old feud between Shaq and Kobe—presented itself after Bryant struggled through his second preseason performance in Las Vegas 24 hours after his Anaheim debut.

On the eve of the season opener, once again there was trouble in paradise.

Taking seriously his role as "Big Dog" on the team, Shaq O'Neal offered some advice that was not favorably received by Bryant. The Lakers' center, through the media, made the suggestion that Kobe "not really do too much until he's ready" and "look to be more of a passer until he gets his legs strong."

It shouldn't have been that big a deal; O'Neal was right. But he was taking a risk in disturbing the vulnerable Bryant, who had never taken kindly to unsolicited counsel— including that which arrived from the locker of Goliath.

"I definitely don't need advice to play my game," Bryant said when O'Neal's words were put in front of him.

"Not even from Shaq?" someone asked.

"Definitely not," Bryant replied. "I know how to play my guard spot. He has to worry about the low post."

Then it was back to Shaq. "If he don't like it," O'Neal said, "then opt out." That was a direct reference, certainly one management would not appreciate, to Kobe's contractual right to leave the Lakers following the 2003-04 season as a free agent.

O'Neal wasn't done pouring kerosene on the flames, pointing out that, in his mind, superstars Karl Malone and Gary Payton had chosen to sign with the Lakers as free agents not because of Bryant's presence, but because of the giant in the middle.

"Just ask Karl and Gary why they wanted to come here," Shaq said, putting the newcomers in an awkward position. "One person, not two was the reason. One.

"As we start the new season, we want [things] done right. As long as it's my team, I'll voice my opinion. Yep, it's my team. You guys might give it to Bryant, like you've given him everything else his whole lifetime. But this is the Diesel's ship, and if we're not right, I'm going to go out there and try to get [it] right."

As if the impending trial in Colorado hadn't caused enough headaches, Bryant was dealing with old business in the locker room, the kind that divided a team. True to form, Kobe maintained that he'd play the game his freewheeling way as long as the right knee—the one surgically repaired in Vail on July 1—allowed.

"Right now my leg won't carry me for 48 minutes," Bryant said. "But I can get in there and do some things, probably. As far as playing a whole bunch of minutes, that's not realistic. I have to be smart about it. I'll continue with my conditioning and strengthening, and let it go from there."

One professional player told a reporter that Bryant's arrest had sent a ripple-effect through the NBA, serving as a warning to other players who were accustomed to "hooking up" with unknown women.

"It's definitely locker room conversation," the player said. "Everyone is a bit on edge right now. No one really knows whether or not Kobe's guilty or innocent – they just shake their heads and say, 'Man, that guy is in a lot of trouble.' He's a phenomenal player and in the past we've all wished we could play like him – but right now, we're all just thanking God we're not in his shoes."

The latest power struggle would no doubt invite more speculation that Bryant would, indeed, opt out of his contract after eight seasons in L.A. and relocate with his old mentor, Jerry West, in Memphis with the Grizzlies. It certainly would be much quieter for Kobe in Graceland than in Hollywood.

During training camp in Hawaii, Bryant mentioned how he was "terrified" for family members and that he worried about the strain this case was putting them through.

In Colorado, and elsewhere, there were people feeling the same way about a 19-year-old woman and her family.

# 15

## HEAT SEEKERS

While Kobe Bryant was seeking sanctuary back home in Newport Beach, his team of personal private investigators were scouring the nation for information about the woman who would testify against him. The investigators, who were financed with almost unlimited resources, were able to exhaust leads more effectively than the Eagle County law enforcement community, who were constrained by bureaucratic budgets.

In November, a number of friends and family members started receiving visits from Bryant's investigators. One such visit was to Lilly's apartment complex to solicit any information that would help in Bryant's defense. Shortly after obtaining a copy of Lilly's work application at Cordillera, one of the investigators tracked down a reference she had listed from New York.

The investigator told the man from New York that he was interested in interviewing him and a variety of Lilly's other friends, namely Lilly's former roommate from school,

Mandy Ross. If they were willing to talk now, the investigator said, they could avoid being subpoenaed at trial. The investigator used an analogy to justify why he should grant him an interview.

"Let's say you were driving down the road and you saw someone with the car broken down and they were hurt," the investigator said. "Wouldn't you stop to help them? Wouldn't you feel that it's your civic responsibility to come forward and do the right thing? This situation is no different. Kobe's hurt—he's terrified. He needs your help. Don't you want to help Kobe?"

Shortly thereafter, another friend of Lilly's received a call in New Mexico. The defense, it seemed, was preparing to interrogate everyone they could. In Eagle, Rachel Yandle had been served a subpoena by Bryant investigator David Williams, to testify at an upcoming evidentiary hearing. Williams asked Yandle a series of questions about her former high school friend, particularly relating to her sexual past. Later, Yandle was interviewed by MSNBC legal analyst Dan Abrams:

*ABRAMS: So tell me exactly what happened. You were subpoenaed. What kind of questions did they ask you? Tell us everything.*

*YANDLE: Well, first, I'm really hard to get a hold of. So he was stalking me for quite a while and he got my phone number from another friend of the victim. And finally, he called me on my cell phone and came over, told me he had to talk with me even though I was told I didn't have to talk to him later on, which I didn't know. He handed me the subpoena and told, well, first started asking me questions, like questions about if I knew her at the time of when the suicide attempts took place and if she talked to me about it. Then he also asked me if, when, the victim and her boyfriend when they were having sexual relations, or if they were having them if they talked to me about them. He asked me if she bled when she had sex, just a lot of personal stuff that he was trying to get information out of me.*

*ABRAMS: Now you say he, this was a defense investigator?*

*YANDLE: Yes, a personal private investigator.*

*ABRAMS: And he said to you what? He said look, I've got a subpoena and you have to answer these questions. How was it characterized to you?*

*YANDLE: He, well, made it, he didn't come right out and say you have to answer these questions. But when he talked to me over the phone, he basically made it sound like I had to talk to him and that he had to give me this thing to come to court. And I've never even heard of having one of these before because I'm not the kind of person that shows up in a courtroom, so I didn't really know what was going on, or why I was getting one of these. But he told me he had to give me one of these and he needed to meet with me. So I figured since he was a private investigator, I had to talk to him. And once he got there, I was actually at my boyfriend's house at the time and he didn't care. He wanted to come over there and talk to me as soon as he could. He even tried to get information out of my boyfriend at the time.*[1]

Abrams then interviewed both defense attorney Mickey Sherman (most famous for representing Robert Kennedy's nephew, Michael Skakel in the Greenwich, Connecticut, Martha Moxley murder) and Florida-based prosecutor, Pam Bondi. Both Sherman and Bondi agreed that there was nothing inappropriate about Bryant's investigators trying to interview Lilly's friends.

"I think it's 100 percent legitimate," Sherman said. "I think it's responsible investigation and preparation on the defense attorney's part. There's nothing that that person said that is in any way consistent with inappropriate behavior. They asked for evidence that's relevant, whether or not this person customarily bleeds during sex. They asked about things about her psychiatric history, I assume designed to

---

1. Copyright © MSNBC, reprinted with permission.

find out whether or not she's someone who is prone to lie or tell the truth."

"They did not tell her that they had to speak to them or that she had to speak to them," he continued.

"It sounds like they did everything right. And I know people don't want to hear that and people want to believe that the defense people are out there, you know, looking under rocks. But don't forget, they are just gathering information right now, Dan. These—whatever this woman says doesn't necessarily get in front of the jury, but it's the responsibility, it's the obligation of the defense people to get as much information as possible."

Bondi reluctantly agreed that the defense had a right to make inquiries but questioned the methods they were using to make them. For one, it was suspicious that the defense was subpoenaing an unusually high number of people. Two, the defense had subpoenaed Lilly's mother, a risky move in the court of pubic opinion.

Abrams was concerned that Lilly's friends might not have known that legally, they didn't have to speak to the private investigator.

"Is this sneaky tactics by the defense team?" he asked. "I mean look, this girl believed—and I'm not saying it's the fault of the person asking the questions, necessarily, but she certainly believed that she had to answer these questions. They make it sound official. Is there any requirement, any obligation on the part of a defense investigator to say, 'look, I want to make it clear. I work for the defense here. I don't work for the government. My client is Kobe Bryant.'"

One of Lilly's friends annoyed by the subpoena was her former college roommate, Mandy Ross. A Bryant investigator had showed up at her apartment and talked his way in by asking questions. Ross was unsure how to get him to leave, and called neighbor Johnray Strickland for help. Strickland immediately ran downstairs and asked security to compel the man to leave. After he left, the young woman called her parents who immediately contacted a lawyer.

Ross wasn't the only one annoyed; Bryant's investigators were equally frustrated. The defense had put together a highly experienced team of investigators from around the United States and they were accustomed to working on high-profile criminal cases. They felt they were acting professionally and appropriately and were tired of having to explain the gravity of the situation to 19-year-olds. In the investigators' view, most of the young people seemed incapable of understanding how deeply they were involved, and it was all the more frustrating to see that they didn't seem to care, either. The investigators were simply trying to expedite an interrogatory process that would be easier for everyone behind closed doors rather than in open court.

"You can take along your attorney, your parents, even the prosecutors," the investigator told Ross. "If we can get this over with now, there's a good chance we won't have to worry about calling you at trial."

When asked by one potential witness what the investigators were trying to get at, one of them simply responded, "the truth."

During the preliminary hearing, Mark Hurlbert suggested that the brevity of the encounter between Lilly and Bryant was a telling sign of sexual assault. As a result, Bryant's investigators tracked down several men they believed had sex with the alleged victim, lining them up to testify that their consensual encounters were just as brief as the one with Bryant. One man the defense located was a college student Lilly had allegedly boasted about sleeping with while auditioning for *American Idol* in Texas.

According to tabloid gossip, Lilly had bragged about the event because the man resembled Justin Timberlake, a popular teen singing idol. The defense traveled far and wide to find every man they could who'd ever shared an intimate moment with Lilly Fuller. The investigators, who were used to seeing betrayal among friends and loved ones, were not surprised that her former lovers were more than willing to talk about her, or that her female friends were happy to lash out at her. In a strange way, some of Bryant's investigators almost felt sorry for her—*almost*.

More than anything the investigators sympathized with their own client. They believed in Kobe Bryant and after spending time with him, they had come to respect him.

*** 

On December 12, the defense filed a motion "to admit evidence of the accuser's purported suicide and prescribed medication." According to the motion, Lilly Fuller was an emotionally disturbed, attention-starved woman who had put herself and others in extremely dangerous situations—including her previous suicide attempts—to win back her ex-boyfriend, Matt Herr.

"The accuser's purported suicide attempts are admissible . . . because they constitute other acts that the defense seeks to introduce for the purposes of demonstrating the accuser's motive, scheme, plan or modus operandi for falsely accusing Mr. Bryant of sexual assault.

"Proof that the accuser makes herself a victim through purported suicide attempts in order to gain the attention of her ex-boyfriend without regard to the harm and worry that causes to other people is essential to the defense's theory that the accuser made false allegations in this case—false allegations that designed, at least in part to attract the attention of her ex-boyfriend without regard to the harm that it caused others.

"The purported suicide attempts are extreme-attention seeking behavior that illustrate the accuser's ulterior motives, scheme and plan to engage in dramatic acts to gain attention to herself—even when those acts are extremely harmful to herself and others.

"The accuser's purported suicide attempts on February 23 and June 30 are admissible because the sequence of events that surrounded the purported suicide attempts is strikingly similar to what happened after the accuser had sexual intercourse with Mr. Bryant. Given this unusual set of circumstances, the purported suicide attempts are highly relevant to establish the accuser's motive, scheme, plan, and modus operandi of creating drama in her life to gain attention."

The motion further named an anti-depressant Lilly had been taking at the time of the alleged rape, which Mackey called an "anti-psychotic medication approved by the Federal Drug Administration for the treatment of schizophrenia." Mackey then cited a case involving a man accused of murder who was diagnosed as a "delusional paranoid schizophrenic." The condition, she indicated, entailed auditory delusions and hallucinations that made it difficult to distinguish reality from fantasy.

When one prosecutor read the motion, he rolled his eyes. He didn't know whether to laugh or cry. In the back of his mind, he could hear Mackey's voice reiterating, as she always did, "I may play tough, but I play fair."

For many members of the prosecution however, "fair" wasn't the word they associated with Pamela Mackey or her tactics. Pointing out the alleged victim's use of a simple anti-depressant, and then suggesting she needed it to treat schizophrenia, was in their minds less than fair. Associating her with a "delusional paranoid schizophrenic," accused of murder, wasn't just unfair—it was ridiculous.

At this point however, no one was surprised. It had become clear to the entire Eagle law enforcement community that Mackey was arguing her case in the court of public opinion and that she was a master of implication in lieu of firm accusation. By the time she was finished, the whole country would think Lilly Fuller was a delusional, paranoid schizophrenic who had framed Kobe Bryant in a desperate attempt to win back her ex-boyfriend.

By the next morning, wire stories and Internet news bulletins across the nation were reporting Mackey's allegations. It would be only a matter of time, journalists' believed, before Mackey would stand before a jury and explain how Lilly Fuller—in her frantic, lonely, distraught state of mind—saw Bryant as a golden opportunity to regain her boyfriend.

Even after Herr had ended his relationship with Lilly in the summer of 2002, she had continued to obsess over him. When the two had occasional reunions back in Eagle, they often found themselves in one another's arms. No matter how hard she tried to defy giving herself over to the one man who had broken her heart, she still could not resist trying to win him back.

But she never did.

What Mackey didn't seem to realize, however, was that by the time she encountered Kobe Bryant, Lilly Fuller had decided her former boyfriend was no longer worth her time. She'd fallen for somebody else.

\*\*\*

Lilly's final encounter with Matt Herr took place on her birthday, June 18. As a reward for her hard work at Cordillera, the hotel granted her a night's stay with friends. As a result, Lilly invited several of her friends from high school to spend the evening with her at the suite. Among those in attendance was Matthew Herr. When everyone left shortly after midnight, she and Herr once again found themselves in each other's arms.

The next morning Lilly threw her incidentals into a small suitcase she'd packed for the night and went home.

Going into her bedroom, she dropped the suitcase next to her bed and climbed under the covers, hoping to get some much needed rest before resuming her hectic schedule.

Twelve days later, when she awoke in a daze after a night in which she'd undergone the most traumatic event in her young life, she reached down from her bed and without looking, pulled the first pair of underpants she saw from that same suitcase. She was tired and upset. She was in physical pain and wasn't quite ready to make a trip across her bedroom to the dresser. And that's how Lilly Fuller managed to shock the nation.

That's why people were left scratching their heads as to how a young woman showed up to take a rape-kit exam in the most incredible case in decades, with intense media scrutiny just hours away, with another man's semen in her panties—a man confirmably not Bryant. Later Mackey would use the discovery to imply that Lilly had slept with three men in three days. Mackey knew that unless Lilly had misled police investigators, it was highly unlikely she'd had sex with three men in three days—there was Herr on June 18, and another man on the 28th—her new secret crush.

Then, two days later, her encounter with Kobe Bryant.

***

Now that Pamela Mackey had suggested the possibility that Lilly had slept with three men in three days, it was up to Bryant's investigators to find the "third man." Initially, investigators suspected that Lilly may have slept with Matthew Herr again sometime after June 28, but before Bryant on June 30.

One reporter who heard about the Bryant investigation tracked Herr to his college apartment via telephone and confronted him about the allegation, but Herr repeatedly stated, "I'm not saying anything," and hung up. The reporter then called the young man's attorney in Denver, Keith Tooley.

Tooley refused to comment, other than to say that his refusal to deny the allegation "was not an admission either." Tooley did note that the question of how many men Lilly had slept with prior to her encounter with Bryant was irrelevant because of a recent Colorado Supreme Court decision. The decision, *People v. Harris*, was authored by the Court's Chief Justice Mary Mullarkey, who ruled that when a person accused of rape says their sexual relations with the alleged victim were consensual, they cannot show that the alleged victim's vaginal injuries may have been cause by other consensual partners.

In *Harris*, the accused was a 43-year-old man convicted of first-degree sexual assault for attacking a 26-year-old woman from Colorado Springs. Like Bryant's team, Harris asserted that his relations with the victim were consensual and that the woman's injuries could have come from sexual encounters with another man.

It was that logic that Eagle County prosecutors had been touting all along, amazed at the nation's fascination with Mackey's suggestions. In their minds, Mackey's question had unfairly prejudiced the victim and did nothing to advance the case. Furthermore, the idea that Lilly had been with three men in three days seemed unrealistic.

Shortly after her rendezvous with the mystery man on June 28, Lilly immediately left town with her friend Mandy Ross and spent the weekend at *Country Jam*, an outdoor country musical festival featuring artists George Thorogood, Tammy Cochran and others. Bryant's defense investigated a rumor that Lilly had "hooked up" with someone during the concert at *Country Jam*—a proposition that Mandy Ross knew was impossible because she and her family were with her the whole time. Lilly didn't return until three days later.

Bryant's investigators knew there was little chance she had slept with Herr again unless it had been sometime after she had left the Cordillera on June 30, the night of the encounter with Bryant, and before she went to the hospital the next morning.

Prosecutors found the notion that Lilly had sexual relations with anyone after Bryant to be highly unlikely, since they found no semen traces on her other than those matching Bryant's DNA. There was however, a small bit of foreign DNA on Lilly's neck that was collected when she was examined by nurses at the Glenview Valley Hospital. Forensic experts at the Colorado Bureau of Investigations told prosecutors they suspected the DNA may have come from an "accidental transfer," a term used when one person's genetic material is transferred to another because of harmless touching, or as a result of clothing that has picked up random hairs and fibers from other clothing while being washed together.

***

When Lilly returned to Eagle on Monday, June 30, she was already late for work. She was scheduled to start at 11 a.m. and it was almost 2 p.m. After a quick change at her home, she hopped in her small sedan and drove to Cordillera. A smile was on her face.

The man Lilly had been intimate with on June 28 was working that day as well, and she'd had feelings for him for such a long time. If anything, she was ready to have a relationship with someone who seemed honest and forthright, someone she could depend on. As far as she was concerned, Matt Herr was history. When she parked her car and walked through the front entrance, her secret crush awaited her.

It was only a matter of time before the nation would learn that the Cordillera bellman, Bobby Pietrack, the prosecution's "invincible" outcry witness, was the man who had been intimate with America's most famous "victim" on June 28, just two days before her encounter with Bryant. Bobby Pietrack, whose credibility would be a lynchpin in determining the believability of Lilly's story, was the man who'd also had sex with her just 48 hours prior. The man the media once called "two miracles shy of sainthood" for his pristine image had made a decision that would affect one of the biggest criminal cases in years.

Bobby Pietrack smiled as Lilly arrived. He was pleased to see her again. Pietrack had always liked Lilly. She had a good heart and he had come to care about her feelings. It would be hard to tell her that what had happened between them would have to remain a one-time memory.

Pietrack had been seriously dating another woman for a year, and although he cared for Lilly, he loved his girlfriend. He'd lost his senses with Lilly, and he knew it. After all, she was attractive and it was hard to work around her every day. But he would have to tell her where she stood in his life. Pietrack worried that before the night was over, she'd be in tears. Little did he know that his prediction would come true under much different circumstances.

Knowing that the alleged victim and the key prosecution witness had slept together, it wouldn't be difficult for Mackey to challenge Pietrack's testimony. After all, who would expect an honorable young man who had just made love to a woman to betray her before millions? And besides, Bryant's investigators knew that Pietrack's relations with Lilly were probably only the tip of the iceberg. If they dug deep enough, they were hopeful they could find something that would damage the young man's credibility and render him useless as a witness to the prosecution. For starters, the investigators pulled every public document available on the family in Eagle. Shortly thereafter, they traveled to Las Vegas where the family was originally from.

During their visit, the investigators interviewed former business associates of Pietrack's parents and compiled a comprehensive file on the family and their history. Although the investigators had covered "Sin City," their most sacred prize was a small piece of information they had learned back in Colorado.

During Pietrack's initial police interview, the college basketball star had been less than forthcoming with detectives about his sexual relations with Lilly. Knowing full well that a pattern of untruthfulness was the most surefire way to discount a witness's credibility, Pamela Mackey was confident the young man would not present her client any serious problems.

Before she would subpoena Pietrack however, she hoped to have her chance with several of Lilly's other friends. Unaware that Lilly had finally lost interest in Matthew Herr, Mackey was hoping to question several of her friends about the lengths she'd gone to get his attention.

None of the investigators working for Kobe Bryant believed that Lilly Fuller had ever once tried to truly kill herself, despite her two "suicide attempts" In their estimation, Mackey was right on track. This was a confused young woman looking for attention by employing high-drama at every turn. She'd gone to extreme lengths to get her boyfriend's attention twice in the past, and now she was simply upping the ante.

Another theory developed by the defense was that there was more to Lilly's circumstances than just drama. Knowing that after she revealed some of the details of the evening in question, she had been lectured by Pietrack's father and endured the panicked cries of her mother, some investigators were convinced Lilly was pushed in over her head. It wasn't uncommon for young people to be convinced that something bad had happened to them by authority figures, and often they would go along just to satisfy their parents or the police.

When Lilly returned to the University of Northern Colorado for the Fall 2003 semester, she didn't anticipate the kind of attention she would receive from her classmates. After being betrayed by several of her friends who sold stories to the tabloids about her experimentation with drugs and alcohol, Lilly's parents and lawyers made a joint decision to relocate her. Realizing that she needed more than just a break from the temptations of college life, the family sent her to one of the nation's top recovery clinics in hopes of rebuilding her self-esteem and confidence.

Lilly had learned a lot from her experience in the Kobe Bryant case. She'd recognized her strengths and her flaws and now it was time to rebuild herself from the inside, to become a stronger person who could fully utilize her talents and abilities. Her closest friends and family had seen her transform into a strong willed fighter who was ready to make her case in court. She had endured death threats, cruel insults and national humiliation and now was ready to use that experience to become a stronger human being. She was determined to make something substantive and meaningful of her life.

Before leaving the University of Northern Colorado, she'd volunteered at the Rape Crisis Center there and even participated in a "Take Back the Night" for victimized women. She was 19 years old and ready to rebuild.

Bryant's investigators wanted to find out anything they could about what Lilly had told others while away.

In 1999, former LAPD Detective Mark Fuhrman published "Murder in Greenwich," a first-hand account of his investigation into the 1975 murder of 15-year-old Martha Moxley. In his account, Fuhrman claimed to have been contacted by a source who attended Alcoholics Anonymous meetings with Michael Skakel, a member of the Kennedy clan. The source, Fuhrman claimed, said that during the AA meetings Skakel confessed to bludgeoning Moxley with a golf club. Shortly after his discovery, Greenwich authorities charged Skakel with Moxley's murder and the Kennedy descendant was convicted.

If Lilly Fuller had ever confessed that she'd framed Kobe Bryant, or lied about what had happened, they were sure they'd find her confession in these places.

They never did.

\*\*\*

At the December 19 evidentiary hearing, several witnesses, including Mandy Ross, Johnray Strickland and Lilly Fuller's mother, were all present with subpoenas in hand, courtesy of Bryant's defense. As they waited in a private room to testify, the defense and prosecution battled over a variety of issues before an audience of several dozen reporters.

One of the most intriguing scenarios was introduced by Judge Ruckriegle who reminded the lawyers that the circumstances were "ripe for new case law." The issue at hand was how to balance the privacy rights of the alleged victim against the "Freedom of the Press" clause of the First Amendment, and the Sixth Amendment rights of the accused to receive a fair and speedy trial.

In the past, the U.S. Supreme Court had ruled that the press couldn't be punished for revealing information about an alleged victim if the press had obtained the information legally. In 1989, the court reasoned in *B.J.F. v. Florida Star* that to punish the press for publishing private information about an alleged victim would create a "chilling effect" on the First Amendment and could impose self-censorship on journalists. Only when there was a "state interest of the highest order," the court ruled, could there be such punishment.

The court's language was strikingly similar to previous constitutional cases in which the court found that there would have to be a "compelling government interest" to warrant censorship or prior restraint. In such cases, the court must examine the issue at hand with "strict scrutiny," meaning it reviews the case with the most intense caution and suspicion.

With exception of cases involving national security and the threat of war, few cases had passed the "strict scrutiny" standard—including the protection of a victim's right to privacy.

And so, after the defense filed their motion to have some of Lilly Fuller's medical records released, a conglomerate of media organizations followed suit by hiring First Amendment attorney Tom Kelly. Kelly, who had represented the media in past Colorado cases made his case to the judge that there were no constitutional grounds for closing the hearings on the issue. Kelly's argument was based on the premise that there was little, if any, constitutional basis for shielding the privacy of an alleged victim against the First Amendment right of the public to hear what was being revealed. Kelly's primary argument was based on the fact that most of the information the media was seeking to have released had already been reported.

"Unless someone gives graphic detail of what's in someone's medical record, I don't think it could be seriously argued," that the hearings should be closed, Kelly said. Legally, Kelly had firm ground to stand on, and Ruckriegle seemed to acknowledge that. Kelly later told a small clique of journalists that he didn't think any major Supreme Court case would make or break the judge's decision and that the argument would most likely rest on a less known state court case.

Shortly after Kelly finished his courtroom presentation, prosecutor Ingrid Bakke told the judge that releasing Lilly's medical records would intimidate other alleged victims from reporting sexual assault crimes because they would fear having their personal medical histories exposed. Bakke said that it was irrational to argue that just because something private was reported, it was acceptable to report it again.

"When the bell is re-rung, it re-victimizes the victim," she said.

Many of the journalists in the courtroom knew that much of the initial information about Lilly's personal life had been reported in the supermarket tabloids. As a result, the tabs had opened the door for the more mainstream media organizations to re-report the information.

Eventually, Lilly's own attorney, John Clune, spoke before the court. It was the former Eagle County Chief Deputy Prosecutor's first opportunity to address the court since his client had been propelled into the case of the decade. Frustrated at the relentless attacks against his client, the young lawyer stood before the court.

Since there was no constitutional standard that addressed balancing an alleged victim's rights, Clune argued that the standard should be, at the very least, the same minimum as the Sixth Amendment rights afforded the accused.

"This is an excellent opportunity to create new case law," Clune said. He cited the Colorado Victim's Right Amendment, which he said was "intended to have some impact, some teeth to it." He then chastised the press for using "information from anonymous sources, and frankly, unintelligent and uninformed sources."

One reporter who was listening whispered to a colleague that Clune was obviously referring to the wave of college students at The University of Northern Colorado who had betrayed his client to the tabloids for money. Although some of the information the tabs had published was accurate, a significant amount of it had been inaccurate, and both Clune and his client were clearly frustrated.

"People don't know my client very well," he said. "She's a pretty strong individual—but there's a certain level of un-enjoyment . . . and discomfort that comes with being a victim and then there's unnecessary humiliation and embarrassment of victims, which is the reason we don't have more victims report sexual assault in the first place."

Bryant's defense had hoped to have nine witnesses testify. Their argument was simple: Lilly Fuller had revealed that she'd told friends about certain medical problems, and therefore waived the doctor-patient privilege.

[They were able to make that assertion in large part because shortly before the hearing, Johnray Strickland contacted NBC and requested they fly him and three friends to New York in exchange for an interview on the TODAY show. He additionally asked NBC to arrange an introduction to actress Neve Campbell, who was also appearing on the show. NBC declined his terms, but did agree to fly Strickland and one other person in accordance with their standard policy. When he was interviewed, Strickland told the interviewer that Lilly was bi-polar.

When the comments were used against Lilly in court at the hearing, her parents expressed concern. Lilly also contacted Strickland and asked him to stop talking about her to any media.

Lilly's attorneys and the prosecution were dismayed at Strickland's comments. They felt that his having discussed her possible medical conditions on air could open the door for the defense to use that against her and allow them to argue she'd waived the doctor-patient privilege by talking with Strickland. In early January, the defense filed five motions, three of which cited Strickland's comments about Lilly's medical condition.]

Clune tried to refute Mackey's request. "Mackey's argument is that if you say you have a medical problem, you've waived that privilege," he said. Clune told the judge that Mackey's argument was problematic, and that the privilege should only be waived when a patient has specifically outlined the nature of the medical problems and what they discussed with their physician.

Throughout the hearing, the defense remained silent. Hal Haddon made one brief comment in response to the prosecution's request to close the medical records hearing. If it were up to Kobe Bryant, the entire hearing would be closed to the public. At that, the courtroom became silent.

After deliberating on the issue in chambers, Ruckriegle decided the issue was of such "significant importance" that it merited a delay in the proceedings. He ordered both sides to file supplementary briefs for an upcoming January 23, 2004 hearing. At that time, he would decide whether the defense witnesses subpoenaed to testify about Lilly's medical history would actually testify. For now, they could go home.

As the witnesses and even some journalists left the courthouse, the hearings continued and were eventually moved into chambers. Bryant, sitting silently beside Mackey, remained motionless for the duration of the day. When he was free to leave, he quickly walked toward the exit, where his security team awaited him.

While Kobe Bryant was fighting for his rights in Colorado, his teammates were in a battle of their own in Los Angeles, against—of all teams—the Denver Nuggets.

# 16

## SMOKE

The young woman in Portland found herself mesmerized by the seemingly endless news coverage. As she sat alone in her sparsely decorated apartment, Kristina Kelley stared at her television and watched as Kobe Bryant strode out of the Eagle County Justice Center under a clear, blue Colorado sky. Outside, the Oregon rain fell lightly on the porch—it might as well have been a million miles away.

*Change the channel*, she thought—*just change the channel*.

But she couldn't. She was paralyzed, as if stuck in a dream. As Kelley watched his tall, slender figure pass through the glass-panel doors of the County courthouse, the sudden jolt of memory was inescapable.

She had tried to forget what had happened that night, but somehow they had found her—and it was clear from their tone that they had no intention of letting her forget about it. It was someone from the hotel where she worked who had put them onto her, she suspected. She had been careless and mentioned the incident to some of her co-workers, and that turned out to be the worst mistake of all.

It was only a matter of time before Kelley heard from the Colorado prosecutors who were attempting to convict Kobe Bryant for rape. They thought she had something they wanted.

One day out of the blue she received a letter from the Eagle County District Attorney's Office. They wanted to talk to her. Eventually, if she said the right things, they would want her to testify. They would want her to come forward and tell the world her story about what happened one night in a small Oregon hotel room between her and a man they were now prosecuting in Colorado.

"No," she had said. She knew how this went down. No.

Kelley found it strange how that word never seemed to resonate with people. It didn't resonate with Kobe that night and now it wasn't resonating with his prosecutors. All she wanted was to be left alone. If she testified she'd end up just like that woman in Eagle—the whole country hating her, accusing her of being unstable and promiscuous, of telling lies and armed with devious motivations. Besides, she didn't feel as if what she had to say was all that important and more importantly, if she did talk it would only be a matter of time before the media would dig up her rocky past as the story's latest feature attraction.

The Eagle prosecutors tried everything they could to convince Kelley to come forward and testify about what had happened that night in a lavish Portland hotel. After they'd sent a letter asking for her help, she became concerned about the path the inquiries were taking. She knew it was only a matter of time before they turned up the heat. She was right.

The next contact wasn't in writing. Though she usually worked in the hotel basement where room service was readied for guests, one evening she happened to be crossing the polished marble lobby when she heard a couple that she had never seen before, asking about her. The man and the woman identified themselves as personal friends of hers, and despite having no idea who they were, Kristina immediately knew "who" they were.

The front desk clerk, unaware of the charade, pointed out Kelley crossing the lobby. They approached the woman and introduced themselves as an investigator and prosecutor for the Eagle County District Attorney's Office. One of them pulled out a small black leather wallet, exposing a gold shield. That's all it took; Kelley turned on her heels and ran as fast as she could across the lobby and disappeared down the service steps.

The next day when the prosecutors ran into her in an elevator, she lost her patience.

"Will you people please stop harassing me?" she said.

"We're just trying to get downstairs," the investigator answered. Kelley shook her head and quickly exited the elevator when it reached her destination. It had taken her a long time to find a good job downtown, and after several years of building a solid work record, she wasn't about to lose it over this.

Later, when the prosecutor and investigator were milling about the hotel lobby lounge, Kelley dispatched another hotel employee to tell them that she wasn't interested in speaking with them. As the investigator listened to the friend explain that Kelley had "nothing to say," he sat quietly and listened. After she finished her plea the prosecutor responded, "If we want, we can compel her to speak in front of a jury—we could subpoena her. We're trying to avoid that."

"Are you threatening her?" asked the hotel employee.

"No one's threatening anyone," said the investigator. "We just want to talk to her and we'd really appreciate any help she can offer," he said.

"She doesn't know anything, she doesn't have anything to say," the employee explained.

The investigator smiled.

"Then there's no reason not to talk to us, is there?" he finished.

The investigator had expected this. There were three of them already—three women who were rumored to have been placed in questionable circumstances with Bryant and none of them wanted to come forward. One of the other women had relayed a story to investigators that deeply interested them. When the prosecutors learned of the details, they believed her testimony would show a pattern of sexual assault. The woman however, refused to testify and told prosecutors that if they subpoenaed her she would not show up. The investigators had traveled to different cities, attended NBA games and watched and waited. They'd walked through the corridors of Los Angeles' Staples Center in hopes that one of Bryant's teammates would turn on him. Eventually, they hoped one of the leads would pan out. Sooner or later, one of the women would come forward, they thought. It was only a matter of time.

When the hotel employee left the investigator and prosecutor, she told Kelley she'd asked them to leave her alone. The young woman sighed with relief. They had tried everything they could. They had tried to break her. They had tried to guilt her. They had tried to make her feel as if the fate of the justice system rested on her shoulders. But she knew that simply wasn't true. This was her time to move forward and forget the past.

All she wanted was her own life—and that life didn't include television cameras, courtrooms or tabloid headlines—because it never would have ended. They would have dredged up her past and made her look troubled and confused. It would have been the death of what little dignity and sense of self-possession she had left.

As a last resort to deflect the prying eyes, Kelley finally told the investigators to call her attorney, which they did. They told her lawyer that they were convinced that if one other woman testified, just one, it would change the jury's perspective in the case against Bryant. "Please tell your client to work with us," they pleaded. "Tell your client to talk with us, tell us what she knows—anything."

A few weeks after the prosecutors left, an investigative reporter from a national news network showed up on Kelley's front door, hoping to convince her to come forward and reveal what had happened to her.

"If I was going to talk to anyone, a reporter is the last person I'd talk to," Kelley told the journalist.

"Then don't talk to me," the reporter said. "Just tell the truth about what happened. I'll respect that."

"I'm not talking to anyone until I have to," she replied. "If I get subpoenaed then I'll testify. Other than that, I'm not saying a word."

"A young woman may have been raped," the reporter said. "A man's life is at stake. This isn't a game. I know that must mean something to you."

"It does," she said. "But what happened between Kobe and I is between he and I—period. It's not anyone else's business."

"It is now," the reporter responded. "They just want the truth. Can't you just talk to them so they understand a little more about what happened?"

Kelley hesitated and then looked into the reporter's eyes as if to convey that she wanted him to take her seriously.

"I understand what you're saying," she said. "I understand why you came here, but you need to understand something. What happened between he and I is between he and I. It isn't anyone else's business. That's it. It's between us."

The reporter nodded, and, as a final gesture that the conversation was over, Kelley extended her hand.

"Just consider talking to them," said the journalist as he crossed the street back to his car.

But Kelley wouldn't talk—at least not with the prosecution. Instead, she had her attorney talk to someone else altogether—someone named Pamela Mackey.

Terrified that prosecutors would subpoena her, Kelley's attorney told lead Bryant defense attorney Mackey that she wanted nothing to do with the case and offered her private assurances that she had no intention of saying anything to anyone about Mackey's client. After all, she had known Kobe for a long time. Everyone makes mistakes.

It was an unexpected move on her part, but then she felt that the prosecution had no choice but to leave her alone. They wouldn't subpoena her to testify if they didn't know what she would say. Now she could be left alone. Now everything would be all right.

But everything was not all right. As she closed her eyes, she could clearly picture the lighting in the hallway that night, the scene frozen in time and space. Kobe had called downstairs because he was hungry and she had brought him something to eat. It wasn't all that unusual when he called back a little later and asked her to come upstairs again. After all, he wasn't exactly a stranger. Throughout the time Kelley had worked there, the two had become friendly. She looked forward to seeing him and they often had pleasant conversations.

Once she was upstairs it didn't take long for them to regain their familiarity with one another. He seemed particularly chatty that night, almost lonely. Come to think of it, she was flattered he'd asked her inside his room just to talk. In a strange way, if even for a few moments, she had felt special. After all, he had needed someone and had turned to her.

He asked her over to the sofa across the room. She managed to hold back a smile. It was amusing to her that he was this bored. After all, there were so many of his teammates in rooms nearby if he wanted company. Then again, he always seemed to be alone. The other players often had women in their rooms and seemed to be celebrating a victory or even a loss. All the while, he'd just stay in his room, isolated from the rest. That's what was so unusual about him, she thought. He was different from the other players who stayed at the hotel. Some of them would find women to spend the night with, even professionals at times. Kobe though, was unquestionably loyal to his wife, all the while exuding a sense of maturity and respect for others.

There wasn't a hint of recklessness in him.

Almost imperceptibly, he moved closer and his arm reached behind her. In the distance she could see the silver CD player sitting neatly on a table with two plastic jewel cases resting against it, the trademark of the hotel's most prestigious rooms. Then suddenly he leaned over and their lips met. It happened so quickly and caught her completely off guard, so she pulled back.

He looked at her, disappointed, and she felt bad. It was flattering at first, however. Here was someone who could have virtually anyone he wanted, but for some reason, he wanted her. She was tempted, but she was already involved. Her current relationship was important to her and flattered or not, she simply couldn't let this happen. As she explained this to him, she hoped he would understand. He had to understand.

After explaining, he sat silently looking into her hazel green eyes. Then he leaned forward and kissed her again.

She pulled back and looked at him in awe. Then he moved forward and tried to kiss her again. He seemed even more assertive, more determined.

She could feel his hand running through her sandy blonde hair. She hurriedly pulled away and ran toward the door. He stood up, but then stopped as she looked back at him. His hands went up as if he were apologizing.

"It's cool," he said, flashing a smile. Exhaling a deep breath, she forced a smile herself and nodded as she turned the doorknob to the room and went out into the hallway. As the golden, brass doors to the elevator opened, a million thoughts were racing through her head. Her hand was trembling and her heart was racing.

As she arrived downstairs, a co-worker came up to her.

"What happened to you?" she asked.

"What do you mean?" Kelley responded.

"Take a look at yourself," the woman said, looking her up and down.

In a nearby mirror she noticed her hair was disheveled as if she just awoke from a deep sleep. Her makeup was askew—her lipstick smeared on the corners of her mouth.

"Something really strange just happened," she said. The co-worker shook her head and began to ask more questions. As she looked down at the floor, Kelley shook her head slowly.

"I don't know what happened," she said. "I don't know . . . he came on to me. He kissed me. I can't explain it."

The co-worker, who suspected that something more than just kissing had occurred, told another employee about the incident. After a supervisor was informed, the young woman was advised not to interact with Bryant in the future. It was better for everyone, they decided. No one knew exactly what had happened on the 13th floor that night and no one wanted to find out. It was best that everyone just forget about it and get on with their lives.

Months later, after having been charged with sexually assaulting a hotel employee in Colorado, Bryant returned to Portland. This time, he was not alone. Neither did he stay in the presidential suite. When they received a call for room service, Kelley noticed that this time Bryant was on the 12th floor. One of her co-workers, who quickly took up the order, was surprised when a member of his security team opened the door. The man quickly signed the bill at the threshold, blocking any opportunity for the woman to enter the room or even see inside. The friendly, high-spirited, optimistic athlete the staff had come to know and admire was suddenly unavailable.

\* \* \*

He'd come in late that night for an early afternoon game the next day. It was April, and all-important playoff positioning was on the line. Everyone was anticipating an incredible clash of the titans—the illustrious return of the NBA championship Lakers to take on their West Coast nemesis Portland Trailblazers.

Portland, used to enjoying a successful home court advantage, was ready.

As Bryant arrived at the hotel, he couldn't help but feel a bit anxious. He could blame the previous losses on the team, but deep down inside he knew he was their clutch scorer. Deep down it felt as if Portland's past victories had been his personal losses.

He was no quitter—and he was no loser either. He would get around it. He would find a way to forget those past losses. As he looked around the hotel room, he realized how empty and alone he was. As isolated as he was throughout his life, he could never quite get over the solitude of being trapped in a hotel room. He needed some company, someone with him, someone to talk to, if just for a little while, to fill that painful void, that silence that echoed all around him.

He couldn't go out. He needed someone to come in, someone he could trust. He could order something from downstairs. He'd stayed there before and recalled a particular young woman who had brought his orders up in the past. Her name was Kristina. The two had become friendly and if he sent for her, he knew she'd come. It wouldn't take him long to start a conversation with her and they would surely have something to talk about. He lifted the phone from its cradle and asked for room service.

Yeah, she'd want to talk to him. After all, he was Kobe Bean Bryant. He was a winner. He was a champion.

His best seasons were ahead of him. This was the game he was born to play, the game of his life. He had at least a dozen years left to show the world that he was the best there ever was and the best there ever would be.

Nothing could stop him now.

# ACKNOWLEDGEMENTS

The authors would like to acknowledge the following:

ABC News
Dan Abrams, *The Abrams Report,* MSNBC
John Alcott, *The Journal News*
Jonathan Alter, *Newsweek*
Roslyn Anderson
The Associated Press
Scott Bauries, University of Florida Law Review
Luke and Starlene Bray
Al Briganti, *48 Hours Investigates*
Michael Cary
CBS
CBS, *48 Hours Investigates*
*The Denver Post*
Daniel Dickenson, Nova Southeastern University School of Law
Andrew Dimas, Santa Monica High School
Joe Halderman, *48 Hours Investigates*
Julie Hayden, Reporter

Neville Johnson, Brian Rishwain and Jim Ryan of Johnson & Rishwain, Attorneys at Law
Lyrissa Lidsky, University of Florida School of Law
Doug Longhini, *48 Hours Investigates*
Joe Marich, Marich Communications
Pedro Malavet, University of Florida School of Law
Robert Moffat, University of Florida School of Law
*New York Daily News*
Juan Perea, University of Florida School of Law
Gerald and Trisha Posner, Authors
Teresa Rambo, University of Florida School of Law
Ron Sachs, Ron Sachs Communications
Eric Salzman, *48 Hours Investigates*
Matt Sebastian, *Boulder Daily Camera*
Rod Smolla, University of Richmond School of Law
Johnray Strickland
Rebecca Tonahill
Michael Tracey, University of Colorado
David Wienir
NBC News
*The Vail Daily*
Susan Zirinsky, *48 Hours Investigates*